ENJOY!

SOPHIE GRAY
ENJOY!

RANDOM HOUSE
NEW ZEALAND

My thanks to Isaac Dunne and family for practising what you preach, to Louie Kennedy for sharing your ideas and experience with gluten-free cooking, and to my long-suffering family who have eaten everything in this book.

www.destitutegourmet.com

A catalogue record for this book is available from the National Library of New Zealand

A RANDOM HOUSE BOOK
published by
Random House New Zealand
18 Poland Road, Glenfield, Auckland
New Zealand
www.randomhouse.co.nz

Random House International
Random House
20 Vauxhall Bridge Road
London, SW1V 2SA
United Kingdom

Random House Australia (Pty) Ltd
20 Alfred Street, Milsons Point, Sydney
New South Wales 2061, Australia

Random House South Africa Pty Ltd
Isle of Houghton
Corner Boundary Road and Carse O'Gowrie
Houghton 2198, South Africa

Random House Publishers India Private Ltd
301 World Trade Tower, Hotel Intercontinental
Grand Complex,
Barakhamba Lane, New Delhi 110 001, India

First published 2007. Reprinted 2009.

ISBN 978 1 86941 909 7

Cover photograph: Aaron McLean
Cover and text design: Trevor Newman
Food and styling: Sophie Gray
Art director: Katy Yiakmis
Props as credited on page 160
Printed in China by Everbest Printing Co Ltd

Contents

Introduction

If I were being really honest I'd have to say that a love of cooking is not my driving force, rather I have a love of eating. I also love my kids, the little horrors, and all the noisy, messy chaos that is family life, and of which food is such an important part.

We are still in the thick of our child-raising years and like many other families we have significant financial constraints. The simple fact of the matter is that despite how much I love to eat good food, I have to watch what I spend, so all my recipes are reasonably inexpensive to make.

And when I refer to family I am thinking about whoever sits around your dinner table in the evening: it may be just yourself and your partner, it may be a passel of kids or flatmates or half the neighbourhood. However different your household looks from mine though, they'll all expect to be fed at some point every day.

If you only ever have the very best of ingredients, it's easy to make something good, but I think the real challenge is making something delicious out of what you have to hand, and doing it again tomorrow and the next day and the next, 365 days a year. Add to that the need to cater for individual tastes and specific dietary needs, within a budget, and you realise what a challenge home cooking is.

Many of the recipes in this book are really easy to make, with busy or beginner cooks in mind. In many cases seasonings can be adjusted, dishes doubled or serving style adapted to suit your family. I have also tried to make life easier for those who have to accommodate food allergies by testing the recipes to see if they can be satisfactorily made using gluten- and dairy-free substitutes as this can be a difficult, stressful and expensive process.

As with all the *destitute gourmet* cookery books I have included some really practical stuff about ways to save money on the grocery bill so you have a little extra to spend on the things that really give you quality of life. But, most of all, I have tried to select recipes that appeal to a wide range of ages and tastes — I hope you find it helpful.

Cook, eat and enjoy.

Sophie Gray

Eat well, spend less

Creating and sticking to a grocery budget isn't a punishment for the sins of overspending, nor does it have to feel like a diet, it's simply a very good choice whatever your financial circumstances might be.

In our family we choose to spend less money on groceries so we have money left to spend on some of the other important things in life.

Using the following three destitute gourmet principles will provide a framework for reducing your weekly grocery bill. The principles have been tried and tested and I am sure that if you use them you will save money, but first 'The Talk'.

Having made the decision to get your grocery spending under control you need more than good intentions to succeed. You need a plan of attack.

Much of your success will be down to moment-by-moment decisions. However, if you feel as if you are on a diet and simply depriving yourself of all your favourite things to the point that you blow out, like most dieters, you will fail.

Also, like a dieter, you will feel depressed, deprived, and resentful when other people are having things that you aren't. Just remember, this is about you and your household. Make good choices about what you spend in the supermarket and you will have money left in the longer term to spend on things that give you real quality of life — debt reduction, education, travel, shoes, handbags . . .

Destitute Gourmet principles

dg principle no. 1
Shop smart

- Shop once a week or once a fortnight only. Take a list (see dg principle no.3, page 9). Avoid the quick dash into the supermarket on the way home — you can never buy one thing in two minutes. It will take at least 10 minutes and you will probably buy five things!
- When you run out of something prior to shopping day, try and make do. Most of us have jars and packets in the cupboard we never empty — use what you have and improvise.
- Buy the supermarkets' own brands for staples, such as flour, eggs, sugar, etc. House-branded goods can save you as much as 10 per cent.
- Shop around — the supermarket is rarely the best value place to buy meat and fresh produce. Find a local supplier for these items.
- Try the Chinese or Indian supermarket in your area — many items will be substantially cheaper than in the mainstream supermarkets.
- Keep a price book — alphabetise a notebook and enter all the products that you usually buy and their prices.
  The price book enables you to accurately determine when something is on special (supermarkets often put little labels up which imply that the price has been adjusted even if it hasn't). When competing supermarket mailers come through the letter box you can choose where to shop. Price your grocery shop before you do it; even cost your favourite recipes.
- Shop with cash — if possible withdraw the amount you would *normally* spend. Anything you save becomes 'grocery surplus'. Put it in an envelope in a safe place. Under no circumstances tell teenagers where you keep it.
- Each week what you save goes in grocery surplus. Use this fund for bulk buying on specials, paying for unexpected expenses, such as doctors, school trips, babysitters, gifts, debt reduction, treats — quality-of-life stuff.
- Avoid semi-prepared products and ready meals. Don't buy *anything* you can realistically make yourself, such as pasta sauces, casserole seasonings, biscuits, muffins, curries, muesli, lunch box bars.

It's expensive to eat ready-prepared meals and nutritionally they have severe limitations. Homemade food tastes better and is better for you but the palates, particularly of young people, have become very conditioned to the flavours and textures of processed foods.

If spending less on groceries is a priority for you then decide now not to buy anything you can realistically make yourself.

Many people are surprised when they realise how much they depend on convenience foods, and have assumed ready-made products are available because they are difficult or time-consuming to make.

While that is the case with some specialised items, much convenience food is simple everyday stuff — pasta sauces, gravies and seasoning mixes, salsas, dips and pastes, pizzas and soups, vegetables and gratins, baked goods and breads, all bottled, bagged, boxed, snap-frozen, tetra-packed and canned for our convenience.

So, why bother making a recipe from scratch?

Homemade food is more flexible than ready-made. Leftovers can be frozen, ingredients substituted and improvisations made to accommodate specific dietary needs. Seasonings can be adjusted to cater for individual likes and dislikes, recipes can be adapted to maximise ingredients that are in plentiful supply, all with the added bonus that the homemade version will often be cheaper, with superior flavour and nutritional value and contain no additives, preservatives or ingredients you can't pronounce.

There are some brilliant convenience foods; e.g. tinned tomatoes, baked beans, tinned sweetcorn, stock, tomato paste and basic frozen veg and I wouldn't be without them as they are inexpensive and versatile. Just be selective.

dg principle no. 2
Eat healthily and in season

- Buy less meat, buy the best quality you can afford and make what you buy go further.
- Learn to cook with pulses and legumes. They are very cheap and are one of the foods nutritionists recommend we eat more of, being an excellent source of protein, iron and fibre and containing no fat. Use them instead of, or in addition to, meat.
- Eat in season — at your local fruit and veg shop the most plentiful foods are likely to be at the peak of their season and, therefore, the cheapest and freshest.
- Store the seasonal surplus by freezing, bottling or even drying.
- Use a fruit and veg specialist — your local fruit and veg shop should be experts in storage so that you get the freshest produce. They will also be able to tell you how best to store your purchases to minimise waste.

Use the carbohydrate and vegetable portions of the meal to make the most of your meat. Serve a family casserole in a ramekin with a cobbler topping or in a pasty, wrap or crust. Fill the plate with inexpensive seasonal produce and you not only extend your housekeeping money, but you also improve your health.

We borrow culinary styles and techniques, flavour combinations and seasonings from some of the best and most exciting cuisines in the world so the dishes are interesting, fashionable and delicious — they are also affordable.

dg principle no. 3
Make a little of something luxurious go a long way

- Make a list of all your basic 'pantry essentials' — the things that keep the family ticking over, such as fresh fruit and veg, staples, basic cereals, bread, milk, dairy products, cleaning products, toiletries.
- Make a list of 'luxuries' — anything you like but can live without, such as ice-cream, wine, fancy cereals, little things to hang in the loo, biscuits, packet meals, fancy oils, etc.
- Check the lists before you shop and buy only one luxury item and one cleaning product each week, and only if you can afford it. You will become far more careful about how you use luxury ingredients to keep meal times interesting, but you will use less.

Having access to your favourite ingredients and foods helps you stay on track — a little treat may prevent a major blow-out later on.

We use our grocery surplus for little luxuries like visits to cafés or child sponsorship, sports and music lessons. Those things may not be a priority in your family, but the grocery surplus can help you identify and achieve what is.

Get the family on board with your budget goals; discuss the benefits of the choices that you are making. If you need to, introduce an incentive to encourage co-operation.

One family I know told the kids that once they'd paid the car bill (a biggy) the rest of the grocery surplus for that quarter would be spent on them at Christmas. At that point they were totally committed to the changes. How much you save and how you use those savings is up to you.

About the allergy options

Isaac is my son Jack's best friend, and it's a *serious friendship*. Serious in the sense that Isaac lives with life-threatening food allergies and everything that goes along with that.

He is fatally allergic to dairy products, eggs, nuts, and some starches, suffers from severe eczema, and is seriously allergic to dust, pollen and pet hair. None of which I had dealt with before we invited this cool kid around to play. He came, with emergency phone numbers, EpiPen and instructions (should I cause him to have an anaphylactic reaction), his ubiquitous lunch box of Isaac-safe snacks and a terrific sense of humour.

It was the lunchbox that got me. Kids hate to be different and food is such a universal, social lubricant that virtually every group situation just serves to highlight their differentness.

Allergic adults miss out on dinner invitations, the work 'do' can be more trouble than it's worth, and they rarely get presented with surprise cakes on their birthdays.

As adults many of the allergy sufferers I know actually become apologetic for their condition — 'I'm so sorry I'm so difficult to cater for.'

While cooking for someone with food allergies may appear daunting, once you have a few basic ingredients in stock you don't need to be intimidated.

The most common food allergies and intolerances are to dairy products, nuts, gluten, eggs and wheat. None is insurmountable but all should be taken seriously.

Whether it's a kids' play date or a dinner party, you can make delicious allergy-safe meals and treats without spending a fortune.

Make sure you:

- ask dinner guests or the parents of visiting littlies if there is anything they cannot eat
- read all labels carefully — even a pack of plain potato chips may contain dairy solids
- avoid using ingredients purchased from bulk bins or mixed display cabinets as there is a high risk of cross-contamination
- take care not to cross-contaminate — wash all chopping boards, knives and utensils thoroughly
- serve the same food to everyone — there is less risk of contamination and everyone feels included
- check with your guests that what you have prepared is safe for them, then you can all relax and enjoy the meal.

Store cupboard substitutes

- Use a dairy-free spread instead of butter. Be certain that it is dairy-free — lactic acid used as a food additive can be from a dairy source or a non-dairy source. Check with the manufacturer if you are unsure.
- Substitute cow's milk with soy or rice milk in baking and sauces — Tetra packs are shelf stable so you can keep a spare in your pantry.
- Use glutinous rice flour from an Asian food store to thicken sauces, gravies, etc.
- Ensure condiments such as soy sauce, Worcestershire sauce, stock and seasonings are allergy safe.
- Keep a bar of allergy-safe chocolate in stock — Kinnerton make one that is dairy-, egg-, nut- and gluten free with 70 per cent cocoa solids. It's great for cooking but also a tasty eating chocolate and is available in some supermarkets.
- A loaf of gluten-free sliced bread in the freezer is a good stand-by for recipes such as meat balls and burgers that use breadcrumbs to bind or extend the mixture.
- Xanthan gum and guar gum are used in gluten-free cooking to help the mixture hold together. Buy it in the health-food shop and keep it in the pantry for when you need it. (Many gluten-free recipes will use it.)
- Egg-replacer products are an allergy-safe egg alternative for baking. Available in health-food shops, they're not suitable for every recipe but can be useful.
- Keep a stock of 'free foods' – in most cases fresh fruits and vegetables, rice, and natural popcorn are safe, cheap everyday foods. A tub of really good sorbet in the freezer can provide an allergy-safe treat at any time.

While we don't live with allergies ourselves we now know so many people who do. Consequently, I've developed a keen interest in this area of family food. Adjusting to life with food allergies can be extremely trying and expensive, so I have tried to make the recipes in this book as inclusive as possible. We have not attempted to do egg-free variants of all the recipes for purely practical reasons. However, in many cases the recipes can be adapted to accommodate other allergies such as to nuts or wheat, etc.

If you have never cooked gluten-free food then, in the words of glutenfree.com, 'you may need to adjust your expectations'.

Wheat flour can't simply be replaced with just any other flour: some flours respond differently under different circumstances. Among the biggest problems with gluten-free cooking are the flavours (a chalky or bitter taste often occurs) and texture (which may become rock hard, gluey or sticky).

As someone who eats wheat-flour products every day I have compared every recipe here with the wheat-flour version and have thrown away batch after batch of bread or baking that didn't feel or taste sufficiently close to the original.

Breads and pastry are the things that most people give up on: I really wanted to produce bread that was gluten free and that my family and I would happily eat and we think I've finally done that.

The plain white loaf, page 12, while small, tastes and toasts like 'real' bread. I sacrificed size for palatability. All attempts to produce the same result in a larger loaf failed miserably. (Tears may have been shed and a bad word or two uttered, but I couldn't confirm that.) The Italian herb bread on page 119, baked in a small shallow pie dish, has the best texture but can only be eaten as a wedge or a finger. If you don't mind eating long thin slices of bread then bake your bread in that type of pan every time.

Both can be used to make breadcrumbs or bruschetta or used for sandwiches and toast. Sandwiches from the little white loaf won't need to be cut in half.

Gluten-free flour mix # 1

This flour mix when used in conjunction with eggs produces a strong enough structure for good bread and some cakes. It has no bitter aftertaste and all the ingredients can be purchased very cheaply from Asian and Indian food stores.

2 cups glutinous rice flour
1 cup potato starch flour
1 cup tapioca flour/starch

Mix the ingredients together and sift into an airtight container to store and use as required for bread, and high cakes that require more structure.

Gluten-free flour mix # 2

I use this as a general-purpose baking flour and add xanthan or guar gum as a binding agent in varying quantities, according to what I am making.

1 cup maize cornflour
2 cups glutinous rice flour
1 cup millet flour
1 cup potato-starch flour
1 cup potato flour

Mix the ingredients together and sift into an airtight container to store and use as required.

Cook's tip

I have recently become a convert to instant yeast sachets, as they simplify the bread-making process. Instant yeast sachets contain active dried yeast in very fine granules that will dissolve and activate in the flour, whereas traditional dried yeast granules are coarse and need to be activated in liquid. To use, simply replace the measure of yeast in the recipe with an instant yeast sachet. Mix it in with the dry ingredients, and any fat or oil. Add the measures of warm milk or water and mix the dough together. Knead well and set aside to rise, according to the recipe.

Plain white gluten-free loaf

This makes a small, easy-to-slice loaf of light crumbly textured white bread. It toasts well, doesn't stale as soon as you look at it and tastes like proper bread.

A dough hook is required to mix the dough. I knead most dough by hand, but this mixture is somewhere between a batter and a dough, so I use the dough hooks that came with my hand-held mixer. Actually, this recipe is the only thing I've ever used them for.

2½ cups gluten-free flour mix # 1
1½ 8-g sachets of instant yeast
½ tsp salt
1 tsp sugar
2 tsp guar gum
1 tbsp oil
½ cup milk
½ tsp wine vinegar or cider vinegar
   (not malt vinegar)
3 eggs

In a bowl, combine the flour, yeast, salt, sugar, guar gum and oil.

Warm the milk — warm, not hot — add the vinegar and eggs and beat thoroughly. Mix into the dry ingredients and knead with the mixer for 2 or 3 minutes until the mixture is smooth and elastic.

Place the bowl inside a clean plastic bag or cover with cling film and place in the microwave on low power (10 per cent) for 1 minute. Let the dough rest for 20 minutes then tip into a well-greased loaf pan. Using a piece of non-stick baking paper, gently press the dough into the tin, trying not to knock all the air out of it.

Cover the dough with plastic and leave in a warm place for approximately 50 minutes — the dough needs to double in size in the tin before you bake it.

I find the dough rises more quickly in a warm, not hot, turned-off oven. (I warm the oven while the dough is resting in the bowl then turn it off ready for the dough once it's in the tin.)

Preheat the oven to 190°C (removing the rising loaf first).

When the dough has doubled in size, bake the loaf for 20 minutes. It will be pale golden — lighter in colour than a wheat loaf — and will sound hollow when tapped on the bottom. Cool on a wire rack.

Gluten-, dairy- and egg-free pastry

This is the pastry we use for all gluten- and dairy-free pastry dishes; it tastes so good no one would ever know its G, D & E free. The dough is quite 'short', in other words it is soft and breaks easily. Consequently, it cannot be rolled out and lifted into position like a regular pastry. Instead, roll it *in situ*, press it into pie dishes or — my preferred method for fragile or sticky gluten-free mixtures — roll it between two sheets of non-stick baking paper then invert it into or onto the tin or tray.

For savoury pastry

125 g dairy-free spread
1/3 cup glutinous rice flour
1/3 cup potato flour
1/2 cup maize cornflour
1 tsp baking powder
1 tbsp brown sugar
1/4 cup water or soy milk

For sweet pastry add

1½ tbsp brown sugar
1½ tsp vanilla essence
a pinch of cinnamon

Mix the dairy-free spread into the dry ingredients then add vanilla essence and sufficient liquid to form a soft dough.

Roll the pastry between two sheets of non-stick baking paper. This pastry can be pressed into pie dishes and flan cases. It can also be used in free-form recipes as follows.

Free-form galette method

Roll chilled pastry out to a 35-cm diameter circle (approximately). Don't worry about ragged edges. Place on a lightly greased baking sheet and preheat the oven to 200°C. Brush the middle of the pastry with egg yolk (optional, but this helps prevent it getting soggy during cooking) and sprinkle it with gluten-free breadcrumbs to absorb some of the juices released by your filling during cooking.

Simply pile prepared filling into the centre; for example fruit, roasted veg with a bit of pasta sauce, leftover casserole — whatever you have to hand.

Fold the edges of pastry in towards the middle but leave an open circle in the top so you can see the filling. Brush pastry with soy milk and sprinkle with sugar or Parmesan cheese.

Strudel method

Roll pastry to a rectangle about 28 cm x 14 cm and lay on a baking sheet. Pile chosen filling mixture down the middle of the pastry and gently fold long sides of pastry towards the centre leaving the middle uncovered. Bake for 25–35 minutes or until pale golden, then cool.

About the ingredients

Dairy-free condensed milk

Condensed milk is used in slices and bars to sweeten and bind the mixture. It also caramelises to make voluptuous caramely fillings. This dairy-free condensed milk is fast and easy to make and has no hint of soy flavour when used in baking. It doesn't caramelise like regular condensed milk but the addition of caramel flavour produces the right result. Lovers of my fudge cake recipe (dg *More Stunning Food from Small Change*) should make it for their dairy-allergic friends using this condensed milk, a packet of Arnott's Nice biscuits (they are dairy-free) and a non-dairy substitute instead of butter. It turns out really well, just ask Isaac. The following makes 1 big cupful (approx. 300g).

¾ cup sugar
½ cup water
1 scant cup soy milk powder —
    I use a product called Soy Drink
    by Herb Valley, available in
    health-food shops
2 tbsp caramel flavouring (optional)

In a saucepan, dissolve the sugar in water over a low heat. Using a whisk, mix in the soy milk powder stirring continuously over the heat for 3–4 minutes, until the mixture is completely smooth and thickened. Add caramel flavouring if using.

Cook's tip

Caramel flavouring or essence is available in supermarkets and comes in a variety of forms. However, some contain wheat so check the labels. I use one called *Torani caramel flavouring syrup*, mostly sold for flavouring coffees (Torani is the brand).

Most of the following flours have ancient origins and have been used for centuries by cultures that didn't use wheat; consequently you often find them in the bulk bins of an Indian food supplier or in an Asian grocery and they are very inexpensive.

Maize cornflour: Yellow in colour, don't confuse it with the cornflour you use for thickening sauces — that is cornstarch and behaves differently. I buy cornflour in bulk from an Indian food supplier.

Glutinous rice flour: Despite the name, this *does not contain gluten*. Glutinous rice, also called sticky rice, sweet rice, waxy rice, botan rice, mochi rice, and pearl rice, is a type of short-grained Asian rice that is especially sticky when cooked. It is called *glutinous* in the sense of being glue-like, not in the sense of containing gluten. I find it performs better than regular rice flour, and is really cheap from Asian/Chinese grocery stores.

Millet flour: Highly nutritious, non-glutinous and like buckwheat and quinoa, millet flour is soothing and easy to digest. It has a mildly sweet, nut-like flavour, is nearly 15 per cent protein, contains high amounts of fibre, B-complex vitamins (including niacin, thiamine, and riboflavin), the essential amino acid methionine (whatever that is), lecithin, and some vitamin E. It is particularly high in the minerals iron, magnesium, phosphorous, and potassium and it produces light, crumbly baked goods.

Potato-starch flour: Not to be confused with potato flour, which is made from potato that has been dried and ground into a powder, potato-starch flour is made from the starch only and works well in combination with other flours as its tendency is to bind rather than crumble.

Potato flour: It's hydroscopic — in other words it attracts and retains moisture — so potato flour can be helpful when used in combination with other flours to produce moist end-products. Also quite dense and heavy, it adds substance when combined with other more crumbly flours and is very cheap from Indian food stores.

Tapioca flour: Made from *Cassava* root, tapioca flour helps to contribute 'chew' factor to gluten-free mixtures. It is more inclined to bind than crumble so it's useful when used in conjunction with crumbly flours.

The all-purpose flour blends in this book use combinations of the above flours, as no single alternative flour will satisfactorily replace wheat flour and these particular flour blends not only produce an acceptable result, but they are also cheap and readily available.

There is a large number of other gluten-free flours to experiment with, including flours made from legumes, such as lentils and chickpeas, finely ground nuts, seeds and roots, each having different characteristics, such as flavour, texture, moisture retention and so on. Soy, lentil, sorghum, brown rice and chickpea are all common in gluten-free flour blends and can be purchased in Indian food stores and health-food shops.

Xanthan gum and guar gum: Most gluten-free flours will require the addition of xanthan or guar gum, which is a substitute binder used to compensate for the lack of gluten in the flour. The amount needed will depend on the product and its reliance on gluten for structure. *

Breads rely heavily on gluten for their structure, cakes to a lesser extent, and biscuits almost not at all. As a rough guide, for every cup of wheat-free/gluten-free flour you will need to use 1 tsp xanthan or guar gum for cakes, 2 tsp xanthan or guar gum for breads or pizza, and 1 tsp or no xanthan or guar gum for biscuits. I generally use guar gum as it is less expensive where I live and easier to source, being readily available in health-food shops.

Soy milk powder: Sold as powdered 'soy drink' in my local health-food shop. I use this to make a dairy-free version of condensed milk — while not entirely the same as the dairy version, it does taste caramel-ish when baked and produces a good fudgey texture for desserts and slices.

Milks: I generally use soy milk as my non-dairy milk. If soy is a problem then, in many cases, rice milk is a good substitute although I find it a little too sweet for savoury dishes. In some cases a dash of water can replace milk without any noticeable difference.

Chocolate: Dairy-free allergy-safe chocolate can be very expensive. I use a product produced by Kinnerton in the U.K. It is guaranteed to be free from allergens such as nuts, gluten, eggs and dairy, it comes in a handy little 100 g bar and is good for eating and cooking. It's much less expensive than other dairy-free chocolates I have seen, but use whatever you can get.

Dairy-free butter substitutes: I use a non-dairy table spread called Olivani instead of butter in baking, sauces, etc. Non-dairy spreads do differ from butter in a number of ways. Most specifically they don't 'cream' like butter when beaten, as they are pre-softened, and they may behave differently when melted. All the recipes in this book were tested using Olivani but results may vary if you use a different fat so a little experimentation may be required.

Eggs: As eggs are one of the hardest ingredients to substitute, you need to understand what purpose they serve in a recipe. Eggs can supply both leaven (rise) and binding, so are included in many gluten-free dishes to provide structure. Egg whites may supply volume and lightness to a mixture and whole eggs add fat, protein, colour, flavour and texture. One egg in a recipe may just be a binder, in which case a simple substitution such as a couple of tablespoons of puréed fruit may suffice — more than one egg, and you are heading into uncharted territory.

Where eggs appear in this book it is because we have not produced a satisfactory result when omitting them. If you want to experiment further with egg-free cooking you could try using a commercial egg replacer or make your own.

MAINSTAYS

Tasty, easy and — as always — affordable . . .

I came across a fascinating statistic some time ago about household menus. The research revealed that the average household operates on a selection of around 11 recipes. Every year or so, without really being aware of it, we give our particular selection an overhaul, ditching one or two dishes, introducing a couple of new ones but generally sticking to around 11. That seems to be about all the average household can manage to shop for, remember how to make, and coerce the family to try.

Maybe you live under the tyranny of the OAFL? It stands for 'official approved foods list'; it is generally compiled by the youngest member of the household and rarely includes the recommended number or serves of fresh fruit and vegetables.

I, for one, am over the OAFL. In our house dinner is dinner, you eat it or you go without. With that in mind I try to choose recipes that we will all like. Not too spicy, but interesting, tasty enough for adults, easy enough for after work and, as always, affordable.

Linda's chicken couscous

If I am making this dish, I skin the drumsticks by gripping the skin with some kitchen towel and pulling it off like a stocking. I then drizzle the pan contents with a little olive oil; it's healthier than fat from chicken skin. My kids can't yet manage to skin drumsticks so they cook them skin on and omit the oil.

Serves 4

8 chicken drumsticks
½ onion, chopped
3 cloves garlic, crushed
1 tsp dried thyme
1 parsnip
1 potato, cut in chunks
1 small swede, kumara or
   chunk of pumpkin, cubed
2 large carrots, cut into chunky sticks
2 cups (500 ml) chicken stock
   (use 1½ tsp stock powder
   per cup of water)
2 tbsp olive oil (optional)
1 cup frozen mixed veg
1½ cups couscous

Preheat oven to 180°C.

Place the drumsticks in a large roasting pan. Add the onion, garlic, thyme and all the vegetables except for the frozen mixed veg.

Bake for 20 minutes, stirring at least once, then pour in the stock and oil (if using) and continue cooking for another 20 minutes.

Sprinkle in the frozen vegetables and couscous then give the contents of the pan a bit of a mix so the couscous comes in contact with the liquid and pan juices, which it will absorb. Return to the oven for a further 10 minutes. Scrape all the nice crispy bits of couscous off the sides of the pan if you are serving it on a platter — I usually serve it straight from the pan and we fight over the crispy bits.

Cook's tips
You can add more stock to the pan if it seems too dry before adding the couscous, or try a splash of wine. Different herbs, such as rosemary or oregano, can be used and it can be eaten hot or cold.

'En croûte' simply means wrapped in pastry.

Savoury pork en croute

Use the leanest pork mince you can get even if it means going to the butcher and paying a little extra. The recipe only uses a small amount and the leaner the better.

Serves 4–6

¼ tsp oil

1 onion, chopped

1 large potato, scrubbed and cut into cubes the size of dice

2 sheets ready-rolled puff pastry (use reduced-fat pastry sheets, if you prefer)

350 g pork mince

2 slices bread, any kind, torn into pieces

50 g bacon, trimmed of fat and cut into small pieces

2 tsp dried sage

2 tbsp Worcestershire sauce

1 apple, peeled and grated

½ tsp salt

1 egg, lightly beaten

Preheat the oven to 210°C.

In a small pan, heat the oil then add the chopped onion and potato and cook gently until onion is soft and potato cubes are beginning to soften.

While the vegetables are cooking, prepare the pastry by cutting a strip approximately 6 cm wide off one of the sheets of pastry. Set the strip aside to use for decorating.

Attach the remaining piece of pastry to the full pastry sheet by brushing a little water along one edge of the full sheet, overlap with the smaller sheet and press in place. Put the resulting rectangle on a lightly greased baking sheet and roll the pastry gently with a rolling pin, increasing the width of the rectangle by about 1 cm.

Combine the pork mince, torn bread, bacon, sage, Worcestershire sauce, grated apple and salt in a bowl. Add the cooked onion mixture and ¾ of the beaten egg (save the rest for brushing onto the pastry before cooking). Stir the mixture thoroughly and pile down the middle of the pastry rectangle, patting and shaping to form a sausage, 1–2 cm shorter than the length of the pastry.

Brush along one side of the rectangle, with water then wrap the pastry around the filling. Don't worry if the pastry only just wraps around. Flip the log over so the join is underneath and tuck the pastry under at each end to enclose the filling. Cut diagonal slashes along the top with a sharp knife and then, using the reserved strip of pastry, cut 8 leaf shapes with a knife. Use a dab of water to stick the leaves in a pattern on the top. Brush the whole thing with remaining egg and bake in the preheated oven for 30 minutes or until pastry is dark golden and meat juices are clear. Rest the log for 5 minutes before slicing and serve hot or cold.

Mediterranean jalousie

Jalousie refers to the appearance of a dish that has been sliced to resemble a slatted blind. This one has been influenced by the flavours of the Mediterranean using tomatoes, herbs and feta cheese.

Serves 4–6

1 tbsp oil plus a little extra
  (for capsicums)
1 onion, chopped
2 fat cloves garlic, chopped
1 400 g can chopped tomatoes
1 tbsp tomato paste
½ tsp sugar
1 capsicum
3 sheets ready-rolled puff pastry
90 g feta cheese
1 handful basil leaves
salt and pepper, to season
egg for glazing

Heat the oil in a small saucepan and sauté the onion and garlic until soft. Add the tomatoes, tomato paste and sugar and simmer for 5–10 minutes until thickened slightly. Set aside to cool.

While the tomatoes are cooking, slice the capsicum in half and remove the seeds. Rub oil over the outside and place under a hot grill until the skin is blackened. Put the capsicums into a plastic bag and loosely twist the end to secure. When cooled, the skins will be easy to slide off.

Preheat the oven to 210°C. Prepare the pastry by cutting one of the sheets in half and attaching the halves to the other two sheets of pastry, creating 2 rectangles.

Place one of the rectangles on a greased baking sheet. Spread with the tomato mixture leaving a border of around 1 cm. Brush the border with water.

Slide the skins from the halves of capsicum and tear the flesh into strips. Arrange the strips over the tomato mixture. Cut the feta into slices and scatter over the filling then add the whole basil leaves. Season with salt and pepper, lay the remaining pastry rectangle over the top, carefully pressing around the edges to seal them, then trim them neatly with a knife.

Brush the jalousie with beaten egg, then cut slices into the top with a serrated knife at 1–2-cm intervals. Bake until golden brown. Serve piping hot with salad and fluffy jacket potatoes.

Gluten free

Make one quantity of gluten- and dairy-free shortcrust pastry, see page 13. On a metal baking sheet, roll out the pastry and trim with a knife to form a rectangle approximately 22 cm x 30 cm. Reserve the pastry trimmings and use plenty of glutinous rice flour to prevent sticking. Gently pinch around the edge of the pastry rectangle to form a small lip. Spread the cooled tomato mixture over the pastry, top with strips of capsicum, basil leaves and crumbled feta cheese. Season. Drop little pieces of pastry trimmings over the top and bake at 180°C for 25 minutes.

Dairy free

Use a non-dairy cheese instead of feta or omit the cheese altogether.

Simple satay chicken

Quick to make, with a satisfying satay flavour and only a fraction of fat, this dish is great week-night food.

Serves 4

2 tbsp sweet chilli sauce

1 tsp grated ginger

1 tbsp soy sauce

1 tbsp lemon juice

500 g boneless chicken breast,
    cut into strips

splash of oil

1 onion, finely chopped

2 carrots, peeled and sliced
    into batons

1 broccoli, cut into florets

3 tbsp peanut butter

1 375ml can lite evaporated milk

1 dash Tabasco or
    hot chilli sauce (optional)

rice or noodles for 4 people,
    to serve

Combine the sweet chilli sauce, ginger, soy sauce and lemon juice. Toss the chicken strips in the mixture and set aside while you prepare the vegetables.

Heat a deep-sided frying pan or wok, add the oil and toss in the chicken, stirring frequently until sealed. Add the chopped onion and cook until onion begins to soften. Add the remaining vegetables, peanut butter, evaporated milk and Tabasco or chilli sauce (if using). Simmer gently until the vegetables are tender. Cook the rice or noodles using your preferred method and serve.

Cook's tip

Buy boneless chicken in bulk when on special and freeze in meal-sized lots. The supermarket base price for boneless chicken is around $15.00 per kg; many other meat outlets may have a base price of between $9.99 and $10.99 per kg.

Jambalaya

I have deliberately kept the spices mild in this dish so it appeals to a wide range of diners. If you like fiery, hot, Cajun dishes, add a dash of Tabasco sauce or Caffe L'affare's Rocket Fuel to your dish before eating.

Serves 4

300 g ham steaks, cut from
  a bone-drawn ham
  (ask a butcher to cut
  these for you — don't use
  reconstituted pressed meat)
1 tbsp oil
2–3 celery sticks, chopped
1 green capsicum, chopped
1 red capsicum, chopped

pepper

1 bunch of spring onions, sliced
2 cloves garlic, crushed
2 tsp Cajun seasoning (see page151)
1 400 g can chopped tomatoes
1 tbsp tomato paste
1 cup basmati rice
2 cups chicken stock

Cut the ham steaks into cubes. Heat the oil in a heavy-based pot and fry the cubed ham until it begins to brown, then add the celery, capsicum, spring onions and garlic and continue cooking, stirring frequently for around 10 minutes or until the vegetables have begun to soften.

Stir in the Cajun seasoning, tomatoes and tomato paste and heat until simmering. Add the rice and chicken stock and simmer until the rice is cooked, approximately 15 minutes. Stir occasionally during cooking to stop the rice from sticking and serve with chunky bread.

Little cottage pies

This recipe makes a regular cottage pie filling go a long way. In our house we greedily eat a whole cottage pie in one sitting, so by making individual ones I can set aside a couple for the freezer – a good meal for the kids for another night.

Makes 18 little cottage pies — allow 2–3 per serving

500 g lean beef mince
1 onion, chopped
¼ cup plain flour
2 cups beef stock
1½ cups frozen mixed vegetables
½ tsp mixed herbs
1 tbsp Worcestershire sauce
1 tsp dark soy sauce
2 tbsp tomato sauce
salt and pepper to season
900 g potatoes, peeled
1 knob butter
⅓ cup warm milk
3 sheets ready-rolled puff pastry

In a medium-sized saucepan, brown the meat, add the chopped onion and cook until soft (you should not need oil). Stir in the flour then gradually mix in the stock. When all the stock is included add the vegetables, seasonings and sauces, a little salt and pepper and simmer for 15–20 minutes, stirring regularly.

While the mixture is cooking prepare the potato topping as follows: Place the peeled potatoes in a saucepan of cold water. Add salt and bring to the boil. Simmer until the potatoes are soft. Drain, then return the pan of potatoes to the heat and dry them off completely; this helps produce fluffy mashed spuds. Mash them with a fork or potato masher until broken up, and then add the butter. Continue mashing, adding enough warm milk to give a creamy consistency. (I use a masher to start with then change to a fork to give the potatoes a final whip.) Season with salt and pepper to taste.

Preheat the oven to 190°C. To assemble the cottage pies lightly grease 12-cup muffin pans and line the cups with pastry by re-rolling the pastry trimmings. Bake in batches if you only have one pan. Divide the meat mixture between the pans and top with the mashed potato, pressing it into place with a fork or squeezing it through a piping bag fitted with a large star nozzle. Bake for 15–20 minutes until pastry is crisp and potato is turning golden.

Cook's tip
The perfect cutter for lining muffin pans with pastry is actually a dumpy 425 g tuna tin. It's worth making a fish pie just to get the tin.

Gluten free
Use 1½ quantities of gluten-free pastry, see page 13, and use glutinous rice flour in the meat mixture instead of standard flour.

Use gluten-free Worcestershire sauce and gluten-free soy sauce.

Dairy free
Use a non-dairy substitute instead of butter, and soy or other non-dairy milk for the mashed potatoes.

Spaghetti with meatballs

Spaghetti with meatballs — it's a meal right out of *The Sopranos*. It's also a very simple, very tasty family meal.

Serves 4

FOR THE MEATBALLS
500 g lean beef mince
3 slices of bread, made into crumbs
1 tsp mixed herbs
1 tsp salt
½ onion, finely chopped
2 tbsp olive oil

FOR THE SAUCE
½ onion, chopped
2 cloves garlic, chopped
1 courgette, chopped into
   small pieces
½ red capsicum, seeds removed,
   chopped into small pieces
2 400 g cans chopped tomatoes
1 tbsp tomato paste
1 tsp beef stock powder
1½ tsp sugar
1 tsp oregano
fresh or dried spaghetti for 4 people

To make the meatballs, combine all ingredients together, working the mixture with your hands. Form into 2.5-cm diameter meatballs.

Heat the oil in a frying pan, add the meatballs and brown quickly. Remove them from the pan.

To make the sauce, add the onion and garlic, courgette and capsicum to the oil in the hot pan. Cook the vegetables, allowing them to soften, scraping the bottom of the pan to release any ingredients adhering to the bottom of the pan. Pour in the tomatoes; add the tomato paste, stock powder, sugar and oregano. Simmer gently, stirring for 2–3 minutes. Return the meatballs to the pan and simmer gently, uncovered, for 20 minutes. Serve with spaghetti cooked according to packet instructions and seasonal vegetables.

Cook's tip
You can add other vegetables to the sauce and if your family doesn't cope with chunky sauces, purée the sauce before returning the meatballs to the pan.

Gluten free
Use gluten-free pasta and gluten-free bread for the breadcrumbs.

Stuffed lemon chicken breast

This dish looks posh and sounds a little complicated but my 11-year-old son, Jack, can make it. Pounding the meat and tying the whole thing up with string may appeal to boys who have shown little interest in cooking so far. The finished product tastes lemony and lovely and would grace any upmarket deli.

Serves 4

3 slices of bread
½ onion, chopped
pinch of salt and pepper
½ tsp dried sage
2 lemons
1 egg
1 whole double chicken breast
   with skin on
4 40-cm long pieces string or twine

Gluten free
Use gluten-free breadcrumbs.

Preheat oven to 180°C.

First make the stuffing by crumbling or processing the bread into fresh crumbs and adding chopped onion, salt and pepper, and sage. If you are using a processor just put everything in together and give it a whiz.

Use a fine grater to grate the coloured part of the skin from one of the lemons — this is the zest. Try to avoid grating the thick white pith underneath the zest, as that part is bitter. Add the lemon zest to the stuffing mixture and lastly mix in the egg.

Prepare the chicken by carefully placing it skin side down in a large plastic bag, arranging it so the meaty side is as flat and even as possible. Cover the meat with the plastic and use a rolling pin to beat the meat so it becomes an even thickness. Concentrate on beating the thickest parts, run your hand over the bag to feel if it has become even. It doesn't need to be thin, just even!

When the chicken is flat, carefully lift it out of the bag and lay it skin side down on a board. Squeeze the stuffing into a sausage shape and pat in place along one side of the slab of chicken, then roll the chicken around the stuffing. When it's a neat bundle with the join underneath, take a piece of string and slide it under the bundle. Tie it up with a double knot — tight enough to hold the roll together but not so tight the meat bulges out either side of the string. Do the same with the other 3 pieces of string, spacing them out so the whole thing is an even shape. If some of the stuffing creeps out of the ends just poke it back in with your finger.

Put the chicken into an ovenproof dish then take the lemon that you grated, cut it in half and squeeze the juice all over the chicken. Cut the other lemon in half. Slice one half into 4 slices and slip each slice under one of the pieces of string. Squeeze the other half over the chicken. Put the chicken in the preheated oven and bake for 1 hour or until the juices run clear. Slice and serve hot with veg or a salad, or cold in sandwiches.

Tray-baked lamb with couscous

This is a tasty, savoury all-in-together dish. You can use any seasoning mix you like — I tend to use a Moroccan spice blend but you could use a Mediterranean mix, Italian, or even Indian flavours if you fancy.

Serves 4–6

1 tbsp oil
allow 2 lamb loin chops per
    person (you can make this
    dish using preformed,
    frozen lamb medallions)
1 onion, chopped
2 cloves garlic, crushed
1 medium kumara, peeled and diced
2 medium potatoes, scrubbed
    and diced
3 courgettes, chopped into chunks
1 tsp oil
2 400 g cans chopped tomatoes
2 tsp Moroccan seasoning
2 large sprigs rosemary
1 cup beef stock
1 300 g can chickpeas, or equivalent
    quantity of home-cooked beans
1 cup couscous

Preheat the oven to 220°C.

Place a heatproof roasting pan on the stove and turn on the element to heat the pan. Add a drop of oil and seal the lamb chops or medallions two at a time on each side in the hot pan. Set aside the browned lamb pieces, reduce the heat and add the chopped onion and garlic — you may need another drop of oil. Sauté the onions and garlic until they begin to soften, then add the kumara, potato and courgettes. Drizzle with a teaspoon of oil and roast in preheated oven for 20 minutes. Shake the pan from time to time to turn the veg.

When the vegetables begin to brown, add the tomatoes, seasoning, rosemary, stock, chickpeas and the lamb pieces. Reduce the heat to 190°C and bake for 30 minutes. Stir in the couscous and return the pan to the oven for approximately 10 minutes. By the time you have warmed the plates, sliced the bread and poured a glass of wine, it will be ready to eat.

Chicken biryani

Biryani can also be made with lamb, beef, mutton, and seafood or as a vegetarian dish. The spices are more aromatic than hot, consequently our current crop of kids in residence aged 15, 13, 12 and 10 all like this a lot — it's not too hot. This simplified biryani cooks in one big pot with very little hands-on attention required.

Serves 4

FOR THE MARINADE
150 g (one small pottle)
    natural yoghurt
2 cloves garlic, chopped
½ tsp ground chilli
1 tsp ground cumin
1 tsp cinnamon
2 tsp grated ginger
500 g boneless chicken meat
    (thigh or breast meat), diced

1 tbsp oil
2 large onions, chopped
2 cloves garlic, chopped
1 tsp turmeric
1 tsp garam masala
½ tsp ground cardamom
4 whole cloves (not garlic cloves
    this time)
2 bay leaves
1½ cups basmati rice
2½ cups chicken stock
½ tsp salt

Combine the marinade ingredients and stir in the chicken. Set aside while you prepare the remainder of the dish.

In a large heavy-based saucepan, heat the oil and gently sauté the onions and garlic until soft. Add the spices, bay leaves and the marinated chicken, stirring frequently until the chicken is sealed.

Stir in the rice, stock and salt and allow to simmer. When the liquid is simmering put the lid on and turn the heat down low. Cook without stirring for 25 minutes then check to see if the rice is cooked. If it is still not completely cooked give it a quick stir, replace the lid and cook for a further 5 minutes.

When the rice is tender run a fork through it to fluff it up then cover with a tea towel until needed. Serve the biryani with chutney and naan bread.

How to cook a chook

A roast chicken is one of the simplest and most satisfying dishes, the house will smell wonderful while it cooks, and once you've mastered the basic technique you can try all sorts of variations.

Preheat the oven to 180°C. Allow 20 minutes per 450 g plus an extra 20 minutes at the end.

Make sure the chicken is fully defrosted. Pat it dry with a piece of kitchen paper and place it in a roasting pan. Sprinkle the bird with a little salt and pepper and put it into the preheated oven.

During the cooking time baste the chicken with the juices in the pan — use a large spoon to carefully ladle the hot pan juices over the whole chicken. This helps it to brown evenly and stay moist.

When the cooking time is completed, pierce the plumpest part of the chicken's thigh with a sharp knife and press the flesh firmly — any juice that comes out should be clear. If there is any pink juice at all cook the chicken for another 20 minutes, then check it again. However, if you have allowed 20 minutes per 450 g plus another 20 minutes it should be fine.

Remove the chicken from the oven and cover with foil to keep it warm. Let it rest for 10 minutes before you cut it up. This will allow the meat to relax and will be more moist and tender to eat.

Roast chicken is delicious hot or cold and served with gravy or chutney, hot roast vegetables, mashed spuds or salad.

How to make good gravy

Packet gravy is never as nice as homemade. To ensure that it is free from lumps use a whisk to mix in the liquid. To make gravy you must use the pan and juices from cooking a roast.

1–2 tbsp plain flour
300 ml (approximately) hot water,
   stock or cooking water from vegetables
salt and pepper, to season

When the meat is cooked, remove it from the roasting pan and set it aside to rest. Place the pan on the stovetop. Tilt the pan so the cooking juices and fat from the meat run down to one end. Spoon off all but about two tablespoons of the liquid.

Place the pan over the heat and when hot sprinkle in the flour. Use a whisk to whisk the flour into the fat to form a thick paste.

Add a splash of the liquid and whisk it quickly, then add some more liquid, whisking until smooth. Continue adding the liquid in this manner until all is whisked in and there are no lumps. Simmer the gravy, gently stirring continuously in circular motions over the base of the pan. If the gravy is too thick add more liquid, if too thin simmer briskly for a minute or two.

Season with salt and pepper to taste.

Cook's tips

Chicken gravy can be a little pale and bland — try adding a ½ tsp of soy or Worcestershire sauce to give it some colour and a little more savoury flavour.

Rubbing the chicken skin with butter before it cooks will make it extra golden and crispy but does add extra unnecessary fat.

Adding lemon or orange segments to the cavity inside the bird will help keep a big bird moist as it cooks.

Herbs and garlic will infuse flavour.

Bacon strips placed over the breast of the bird will keep it moist and flavoursome.

Marinades and barbecue-style sauces will all add variety to a roasted bird, or try dry spice rubs and some liquid in the pan while the bird cooks — you could use stock, wine, or a combination.

COMFORT FOOD

Brings solace, soothes and cheers . . .

Comfort, according to the dictionary at least, is 'something that brings relief from affliction and grief'. It is 'a state of ease, a thing or event that brings solace, something that affords physical relaxation, that soothes and cheers'.

What kind of food is comfort food then? For me it has to slip down easily! It's the kind of dish you can eat from a bowl perched on your knee on a cold wet Sunday afternoon, Monopoly spread on the floor, warm socks and a steaming mug of hot chocolate at hand. Or it's a meal that you scoff while snuggled in front of a fire, feet up, watching an old movie with the kids. Nothing that requires the use of both knife and fork!

Comfort food in its truest sense is the tray that arrives on your doorstep the day of your mother's funeral with a meal, a cake, a card and something for the kids' lunchboxes — bringing relief from affliction and grief, providing solace, it is soothing and cheering.

In nutrition terms we are talking starchy carbohydrates: bread, potatoes, pasta, rice and flour. There is something about these foods that just makes us feel cosseted.

Not all comforting foods require hours of slow cooking either. Several of the following main-course dishes can be ready in less than half an hour, leaving plenty of time to make a dessert.

Cowboy casserole

I originally developed this recipe as a simple main course that kids could manage to make themselves. Since then, I've found teenagers, husbands, beginners and experienced cooks alike all like making it because it's easy, pretty quick, uses ingredients that are always in stock and, best of all, it's really tasty.

Serves 4–6

500 g lean beef mince
½ onion, chopped
2 420 g cans baked beans
½ tbsp Worcestershire sauce
½ tsp ground cumin
¼ tsp chilli powder
pinch of oregano
1 heaped tbsp tomato paste
1 tsp beef stock powder or
   1 beef stock cube
1 cup macaroni, cooked
   and drained
1 cup grated cheese

Preheat the oven to 180°C.

Heat a medium-sized saucepan, add the meat and stir until browned, then add the onion and keep stirring until it softens. Mix in the baked beans, the sauce, spices, oregano and tomato paste and sprinkle in the stock powder. Mix really well, then add the cooked macaroni.

Pour the whole lot into an ovenproof casserole dish and cover with the grated cheese.

Heat in the oven until the cheese is melted and turning brown. Serve with salad or veg and garlic bread.

Gluten free
Check that Worcestershire sauce and stock and seasonings are gluten free. Use gluten-free macaroni, penne or other small pasta shapes.
Dairy free
Replace the cheese on top with grated soy mozzarella or omit the cheese altogether.

Chicken and sausage gumbo

This is a really savoury, mildly spicy dish. If the family don't like the little bit of zing from chorizo you could use a different type of sausage or a couple of rashers of bacon. You can simmer the chicken the night before and store in the refrigerator.

Serves 6–8

FOR THE CHICKEN

1 family-sized whole chicken
1 whole onion, peeled
10 peppercorns
1 handful of celery leaves
1 tsp salt
water to cover

FOR THE GUMBO

1 tbsp butter
1 onion, chopped
1 large celery stalk, chopped
2 carrots, peeled and diced
   into small cubes
1 clove garlic, finely chopped
1½ chorizo, chopped into
   small pieces
1 tbsp curry powder
1 heaped tsp paprika
½ cup flour
3 litres stock, from cooking
   the chicken
1 400 g can chopped tomatoes
1¼ cups long-grain rice
chopped parsley or coriander,
   to garnish

To cook the chicken, place the whole chicken in a large stockpot with the onion, peppercorns, celery leaves, salt and enough water to cover the chicken — at least 3.5 litres.

Bring to the boil then simmer for 1 hour until the chicken is very tender. Remove the chicken from the pot and allow to cool. When cold remove the skin and shred the meat, setting it aside to add to the gumbo at the end of the cooking time.

Strain the stock into a bowl. Don't strain it down the sink — you will need approximately 3 litres for the gumbo.

When the stock is cool, skim the fat off the top with a spoon. The chicken can be cooked a day ahead and the stock refrigerated overnight. The fat will then solidify and can be lifted off with a spoon.

To prepare the gumbo, heat the butter in a large saucepan and sauté the onion, celery, carrot and garlic until soft. Add the chopped chorizo, spices and flour then gradually mix in the stock, stirring constantly. When all the stock has been added, pour in the tomatoes and simmer for 15 minutes. Add the rice and stir frequently for a further 15–20 minutes. When the rice is plump and tender add the shredded chicken. Serve in bowls with chunky bread.

This dish can be garnished with chopped parsley or coriander and a sprinkle of paprika.

Cook's tip

Put the stock in the fridge until the fat solidifies and you will be able to lift it off the surface of the stock easily with a spoon. I use basmati rice for this dish.

Gluten free

Use glutinous rice flour and gluten-free sausages.

Dairy free

Use a non-dairy substitute instead of butter.

Flaky fish, caper and lemon pasta bake

We like this pasta bake because it's not cloyingly creamy or cheesy. It's quick and easy to make and goes well with salad in the summer or hot veg in the winter. My husband Richard calls it 'Boy Food'.

Serves 6

FOR THE PASTA BAKE

2 cups uncooked pasta,
    such as penne, macaroni
    or spirals
400 g flaky fish, such as
    cod or hoki
500 ml milk
25 g butter
1 small onion, chopped
1 clove garlic, chopped
1 stick celery, finely chopped
$1/3$ cup flour
1 tbsp capers, chopped
zest and juice of 1 lemon
1 tbsp chopped parsley
salt and pepper, to season

FOR THE TOPPING

3 slices bread, made
    into breadcrumbs
2 tbsp grated Parmesan cheese
a little extra butter, for
    dotting on top

Preheat the oven to 180°C.

To prepare the pasta, fill a large pan with water and put it on to boil. Salt the water then boil the pasta according to the packet instructions.

Place the fish and the milk in a saucepan and heat gently, cooking the fish until done, approximately 5–10 minutes, depending on the thickness of the fillets. Try not to let the milk boil or it will stick to the bottom of the pan and burn. When the fish is cooked, drain the milk into a jug and set the fish aside.

While the pasta is cooking, melt the butter in the pan the fish was cooked in and add the onion, garlic and celery and sauté until vegetables are soft. Drain the cooked pasta and set aside.

Using a whisk, stir the flour into the cooked vegetables, then gradually add the milk a little at a time, stirring well after each addition so the flour and butter roux dissolves into the sauce — the only lumps should be lumps of vegetable. Add the chopped capers, lemon zest and juice, and parsley, and season with salt and pepper. Break up the fish with a fork and fold the fish and cooked pasta through the sauce.

To make the topping, combine the breadcrumbs and grated Parmesan and sprinkle over the pasta to make a thick crust. Dot the top with a little butter and bake in the oven for 20–30 minutes, until crispy and golden.

Gluten free
Use gluten-free pasta and breadcrumbs, and thicken sauce with glutinous rice flour.
Dairy free
Use non-dairy spread instead of butter and non-dairy milk to make the sauce.

Mexican spiced tomato soup

Mexican flavours are very popular with all ages. In this dish the spices are mild and tasty rather than hot and if you want more zing, simply add more chilli. As it is, our kids love this one-pan meal with cheesy scones or bread to dunk in it.

Serves 4–6 as a meal with bread

2 tbsp olive oil
2 onions, chopped
3 cloves garlic, chopped
3 tsp Mexican seasoning
    (see page 151)
2 400 g cans chopped tomatoes
6 cups beef stock (if using powder,
    allow 1 heaped tsp per cup
    of water)
1/3 cup tomato paste
1½ cups red lentils
2 tbsp brown sugar
½ cup chopped fresh coriander or
    parsley
sour cream, to garnish (optional)

In a large saucepan, heat the oil and add the onions and garlic. Cook until light golden. Mix in the Mexican seasoning then add tomatoes, stock, tomato paste, lentils and sugar. Bring to the boil and stir, then reduce the temperature and simmer for 45 minutes. Add chopped fresh herbs and garnish with a dollop of sour cream.

Cook's tip

Mexican seasoning mix can also be used to season mince or added to potato wedges or refried beans for an authentic Mexican flavour.

Red lentils cook
quickly, giving
this soup a thick
satisfying, hearty
character . . .

Make this oh-so-easy stew any time you want tasty, fragrant food you can mop up with a slice of bread . . .

Spicy fish stew with beans and bread

Really good fish is pricy so the trick is to make something tasty from what you can afford. I usually use a cheaper, flaky fish, such as red cod or hoki, but if you have something better use it.

Serves 4

2 tbsp olive oil

1 red onion, chopped

2 cloves garlic, chopped

½ cup white wine
(usually sloshed from
the cook's glass)

1 dried chorizo sausage
cut in thickish slices
(approximately ½ cm)

1 cup fish stock

1 400 g can chopped tomatoes

1 large handful chopped parsley

1 bay leaf

1 dried chilli, chopped

450 g flaky white fish, cut in
chunks about the same size
as the sausage chunks

1 400 g can cannellini beans
(or similar white beans)

8 small mussels (optional)

1 handful black olives

crusty bread, to serve

In a medium-sized saucepan, heat the oil and add the chopped onion and garlic. Cook until soft. Add the wine and simmer until reduced by half then add the chorizo and fish stock and simmer again until reduced by one-third.

Mix in the tomatoes, parsley, bay leaf and dried chilli and simmer for 10 minutes with the lid off.

Gently mix in the fish and beans then cook for a further 8–10 minutes. Try not to stir the mixture too much at this stage as the fish will break up and the soft tender beans will mash. (Too bad, if they do— it'll still taste lovely.)

If using mussels, place the cleaned mussels into the stew then put the lid on for a few minutes until they open. Toss in olives and serve in warmed shallow bowls with a chunk of bread to mop up the juices.

You can also serve the stew over rice or couscous if you prefer.

Friary lentil soup

This rustic soup is thick and delicious, takes very little time and is very cheap. We often intend to include more pulses and whole grains in our daily diet but fail to do so — this dish has all the ingredients that we are supposed to eat more of, so give it a try.

Serves 4 as a main course with bread

2 fat rashers good bacon,
  rind removed
1 tbsp olive oil
2 celery stalks, finely chopped
1 carrot, peeled and finely chopped
1 onion, finely chopped
1 clove garlic, crushed
1 400 g can tomatoes
1 tbsp tomato paste
1 pinch sugar
1 litre chicken stock
1 cup uncooked brown lentils
1 large sprig rosemary

Chop the bacon into small pieces. Heat the oil in a large saucepan and add the chopped vegetables, garlic and the bacon pieces. Cook gently until the bacon is cooked and the vegetables are beginning to soften. Stir in the tomatoes, tomato paste and pinch of sugar and then mix in the stock. When the stock is simmering add the lentils and rosemary and continue to cook for approximately 35–40 minutes, until the lentils are plump and tender, the vegetables soft and your mouth is watering. Serve with a chunk of cheesy bread.

Gumbo with vegetables, coconut and ginger

Most of the spices in this dish are fragrant rather than hot. The ginger and coconut cream give it a lovely exotic flavour and it's really easy to make.

Serves 8

2 tbsp oil
1 onion, chopped
2 cloves garlic, chopped
2 tsp yellow mustard seeds
2 tsp garam masala
2 tsp ground cumin
2 tsp ground coriander
2 tsp fresh ginger
2 400 g cans chopped tomatoes
2 cups vegetable or chicken stock
1 cup small-diced pumpkin
   or kumara
2 cups green veg, such as peas,
   courgettes and spinach
2 cups cauliflower florets
2 400 g cans chickpeas or
   equivalent quantity of
   home-cooked chickpeas
1 330 ml can coconut cream

Heat oil in a large pan and sauté onion and garlic, add the mustard seeds and cook until they are popping, then add all the other spices, coriander and ginger.

Mix well and add the tomatoes, stock, prepared vegetables and chickpeas and simmer approximately 50 minutes, until all the vegetables are tender.

Stir in the coconut cream and serve.

Peach cobbler

I believe cobbler got its name because it bears some vague resemblance to a cobbled street, which really doesn't do it justice. If I tell you instead that it's really easy, you can use any fruit you like and it tastes great warm or cold, you are far more likely to try it.

Serves 4–6

4 large ripe peaches or
   other soft fruit
1 cup sugar
1 tsp cinnamon
1½ cups flour
2 tsp baking powder
½ tsp salt
100 g butter, melted
½ cup milk
1 egg
extra sugar, for sprinkling
icing sugar, to dust

Preheat the oven to 200°C. Grease an ovenproof dish or pie dish.

Wipe the peaches then halve and remove stones. Slice the fruit and place in a bowl with half the sugar and half the cinnamon.

In a large bowl, combine the remaining dry ingredients.

In another bowl, whisk together the melted butter, milk and egg and stir into the dry ingredients to form a stiff batter. Spread half the batter in the dish, add the sliced peaches then spread over the remaining batter. If it is uneven and lumpy with the odd bit of peach showing through, that will just add to its charm. Sprinkle with a little granulated sugar then bake for 40–50 minutes, until golden and springy. A knife inserted into the centre should come away clean. Dust with icing sugar to serve.

Gluten free
Use gluten-free flour mix # 2, see page 12.

Dairy free
Use a non-dairy substitute instead of butter. Use soy or rice milk instead of cow's milk.

Rhubarb fool

Fool can be made with virtually any tart fruit and cream. It is simple and delicious on its own or it can be used as a layer in a trifle or parfait. The light silky texture slips down easily and the sharpness of the fruit ensures that it's not sickly.

Rhubarb fool is my favourite and is so easy the kids can make it next time their grandparents are coming for dinner.

300 g rhubarb, cleaned and
   cut into short pieces
¼ cup orange juice
   (approximately the juice
   of 1 orange)
¼ cup sugar (more, if required)
150 ml cream, whipped
1 egg white, beaten to soft peaks

In a small saucepan, combine the rhubarb, juice and sugar and heat gently, simmering until the rhubarb is tender. Taste and add more sugar, if required. Set aside to cool.

Using a metal spoon gently fold the cream and egg white together, then fold in the cooled rhubarb. Spoon into wine glasses or small dessert dishes and refrigerate until ready to serve.

Cook's tip
Serve fools with biscotti or shortbread, or sprinkle with toasted nuts or muesli if you like a little crunch.

Not so humble crumble

Use whatever fresh, stewed, preserved, canned or frozen fruit you have to hand. Place fruit in an ovenproof dish, sprinkle, spread or pack in the crumble mixture of your choice then bake in a preheated oven until crumble mix is golden and filling is piping hot.

Basic crumble topping

1 cup self-raising flour
½ cup brown sugar
3 tbsp butter

Preheat the oven to 180°C.
Combine the ingredients in a bowl or processor, rub together or pulse to form a crumbly mixture. Sprinkle on top of prepared fruit and bake for 35–40 minutes, until lightly browned.

Spiced almond crumble

1 cup rolled oats
½ cup brown sugar
½ cup sliced almonds
1 teaspoon ground cinnamon
75 g butter, melted

Preheat the oven to 180°C.
Combine the dry ingredients in a bowl then mix the melted butter through the mixture. Sprinkle on top of prepared fruit and bake for 35–40 minutes, until lightly browned.

Coconut honey crumble

1¼ cups rolled oats
½ cup shredded coconut
2 tbsp brown sugar
¼ tsp ground cinnamon
2 tbsp honey
75 g butter

Preheat the oven to 180°C.
Combine the dry ingredients in a bowl, melt the honey and butter and stir through the mixture. Sprinkle on top of prepared fruit and bake for 35–40 minutes, until lightly browned.

Cook's tip
Double the crumble mix and freeze half for another time.
Dairy free
Use a non-dairy substitute instead of butter.

PIZZA, PASTA AND RISOTTO

My best trick with dough is making a little bit of something go a long way . . .

I've tried to make a pizza base by spinning the dough on my fingertips as I've seen on the telly, but I just end up with a giant, squishy, dough bangle stuck around my armpit.

My best trick with dough is making a little bit of something go a long way.

OK, it's not as flash as the Italian dough-throwing, and not nearly as entertaining for the children, but when it comes to producing a meal from what I have to hand, it's proved far more helpful than any amount of culinary juggling.

Whether the dough is rolled into a spianata, stuffed as a calzone or open topped in the more common manner, homemade pizza-style dishes are good food. The crust is low in fat, and the toppings are simply a selection of whatever is in the fridge, with plenty of real vegetables — grated, roasted or just piled on.

We use Edam as our main cooking cheese. Granted, it tastes like a string vest, but it has the advantage of containing 30 per cent less fat than good cheddar. To compensate for the dodgy flavour, I always include a good grating of Parmesan, and there have never been any complaints.

Even I have days, however, when I can't face the floury, choppy, sprinkly, gratey, messiness of pizza. So, rather than making an emergency dash to the supermarket or chippy when inspiration fails, I check out my pantry staples. With a bag of arborio rice a quick, creamy risotto is a possibility. If time is short, dried or frozen pasta is always an option.

Pasta and risotto both start with the 'Italian Trinity' — olive oil, onions and garlic. After that, you can build a meal around whatever is available; for example, a couple of rashers of good bacon, a spicy sausage, a little bit of seafood or last night's leftovers with fresh seasonal vegetables, all gently simmered together to allow the flavours to develop.

Some people consider this type of cooking to be 'café food', but I think of it as tasty, easy, affordable food that I can manage to make on a week night. Give the recipes a try yourself and see what you think.

Pappardelle with crumbled sausage and lemon

This recipe makes it possible for a small amount of good-quality sausage to serve a hungry family. You could use cream in place of lite evaporated milk, if you prefer, and choose a spicy or gourmet sausage. The quality of the sausages is all-important — don't attempt to do this with pre-cooked barbecue sausages or sizzlers.

Serves 4

pappardelle, or other fresh ribbon
    pasta, enough for 4 people
½ tbsp olive oil
3 good-quality sausages (I use
    Italian-flavoured beef sausages)
2 cloves garlic, crushed
1 375 g can lite evaporated milk
grated zest of 1 large lemon
1 handful parsley, chopped

Bring a large pot of water to the boil and cook the pasta according to packet instructions.

Heat the oil in a shallow frying pan, chop one end off each of the sausages and squeeze the meat into the pan. Break the sausage meat up with a fork so it is in crumbly chunks, add the garlic and cook gently, stirring frequently to prevent the sausage from sticking and to crumble the meat as it cooks. When the meat is well browned, pour off any excess fat in the pan and add the evaporated milk. Simmer gently until reduced by one-quarter, then add the lemon zest and parsley.

When the pasta is ready, drain well and add to the sauce. Serve immediately.

Cook's tip

If your pasta sauce has ended up reducing more than you intended, add a splash of the water the pasta was cooked in. The starchy water will extend the sauce and improve the texture.

Chicken fettuccine with asparagus and roasted mushrooms

This is a very simple dish to make as everything bar the pasta is cooked in the same pan. I use a small metal pan, about the size of a pie dish, that can go in the oven and on the element. The sweet nuttiness of the roasted mushrooms is an excellent foil for the fresh flavour of the asparagus.

Makes 2 generous serves

1 single boneless chicken breast, skin on
1 cup whole button mushrooms
1 bunch asparagus
fettuccine or spaghetti, enough for 2 people
1 fat clove garlic, finely chopped
1 slice bread, made into fresh breadcrumbs
1 cup real chicken stock
3 tbsp fresh cream (approximately)

Preheat the oven to 180°C.

Place the chicken in a pan in the oven and bake. Once the meat juices begin to run, toss in the mushrooms, coating them lightly, and continue to roast 15–20 minutes, until the mushrooms are tender. Remove the mushrooms and set aside. Continue cooking the chicken until done.

While the chicken is cooking, rinse the asparagus and trim by snapping off the ends of the stalks. Cook in boiling water for 3 minutes, drain and cut into short pieces.

Cook the pasta in boiling, salted water then drain and set aside. When the chicken is done, remove from the pan, discard the skin and slice the meat. Do not wash the pan. Place it on the stovetop over a medium heat and add the garlic and breadcrumbs, stirring frequently, toasting the crumbs in the chickeny, garlicky pan until lightly browned. Pour into a bowl and set aside.

Return the pan to the heat and add chicken stock and simmer until reduced by half. Add the cream, chicken, asparagus and mushrooms.

Toss in the cooked pasta, stirring it through the sauce. Divide between two bowls and sprinkle with the garlic-toasted crumbs. Serve with crusty bread for mopping up any remaining sauce.

Gourmet pizza with garlic mushrooms and chorizo

Compared with a delivery pizza, this pizza is at least one-third bigger than a bought one and costs $12.00 — that's about $3.00 cheaper than a gourmet pizza from a pizza chain. It takes about 40 minutes to make a pizza from scratch. The pizza delivery companies I spoke to said to allow 30 minutes for delivery and have a minimum charge of $15.00 for delivery. That's a fair amount of grocery surplus!

FOR THE BASE

2 heaped cups plain flour
1 tsp sugar
½ tsp salt
1 sachet instant yeast
1 tbsp oil
⅓ cup milk
⅔ cup hot water

FOR THE TOPPING

1 capsicum
oil for brushing
4 large field mushrooms
   (or 1–2 cups button mushrooms)
1 tbsp butter, melted and mixed with
   2 cloves garlic, crushed
¾ cup chutney
1 130 g can tomato paste
100 g cheddar cheese, grated
2 dried chorizo, sliced into thin
   diagonal slices
100 g feta cheese (the supermarket
   deli sells small amounts if you
   don't want a block), crumbled
fresh basil leaves (optional)

Cook's tip

For a cheaper but still very tasty option, use ham or salami instead of chorizo.

Preheat the oven to 200°C.

To make the base, combine the flour, sugar, salt, yeast, oil, milk and water in a large bowl. Mix to form a dough then knead on a floured bench for 5 minutes, until smooth, springy and elastic. Dust the dough with flour, as required, during kneading.

Place the dough into a clean greased bowl and cover with greased cling film. Place the dough into a microwave and heat on low power (10 per cent) for 1 minute, rest for 10 minutes then repeat, until dough has doubled in size.

To make the topping while the dough is rising, cut the capsicum in half, remove the seeds and brush lightly with oil. Place into the heated oven until the skins blacken and blister, then remove and put into a plastic bag. When cool slip off the skins and slice the flesh into strips.

Chop the mushrooms into chunks and drizzle with the garlic butter.

In another small bowl, mix together the chutney and tomato paste.

When the dough has doubled in size, punch it down, roll out and slip onto a baking tray. Spread with the chutney and tomato paste mixture then sprinkle on the grated cheddar, garlic mushrooms and the slices of chorizo. Lastly add the roasted capsicum, crumbled feta and a handful of fresh basil leaves, if using.

Allow the dough to rise a little, then bake in the preheated oven for 15 minutes, until the dough is golden and the topping piping hot.

Gluten free

Use the plain white gluten-free bread recipe to make the base, see page 12. Instead of pressing the dough into a loaf tin, press it onto a greased metal baking tray and place a sheet of non-stick baking paper over the top. Roll the dough to the desired shape and size. (Small bases could be frozen at this stage — the yeast can remain alive in the frozen dough for about 3 weeks.) Remove the paper and let the dough rise to double its previous thickness then gently apply the toppings to avoid knocking the air out. Bake according to the regular recipe.

Lonely sausage risotto

One sausage and four mouths to feed — this risotto was an adventure that left us all smiling, it was so tasty, not to mention cheap, easy and filling. Desperation dining at its best.

Serves 4

1 tbsp olive oil
1 onion, chopped
1 clove garlic, chopped
3 rashers bacon
1½ cups arborio rice
1½ litres chicken stock
1½ cups broccoli florets
1 cooked cold sausage,
    chopped into little pieces
½ cup grated cheese

Heat the oil in a medium-sized saucepan and sauté the onion and garlic. Add the bacon and sauté until soft. Stir in the arborio rice, stirring frequently until coated in the pan oils. Add the stock a ladle at a time, stirring well and allowing the stock to be absorbed before each addition. When a quarter of the stock has been added toss in the broccoli and the sausage. Continue adding stock and stirring until the rice has swelled and thickened and the risotto is a creamy texture. Stir in the grated cheese and serve immediately.

Cook's tips

One or two good-quality meat sausages will flavour a whole risotto, cassoulet or pasta sauce and produce a much tastier result than any number of cheap pre-cooked sausages — for adding flavour, quality more than quantity is the key with sausage.

Day-old risotto moulds nicely into timbales. Lightly oil a small cup or pottle, pack the risotto in firmly and turn out onto the plate.

Leftover risotto can be shaped into risotto cakes — dip in flour, egg and breadcrumbs and panfry to serve with salad and a relish or chutney as a meal or starter.

Dairy free

Use a soy cheese, such as soy mozzarella.

Cannelloni for a crowd

This recipe makes a roasting pan full of savoury cannelloni. It's a lot less fiddly than it looks and is ideal for a hungry crowd. Halve the mixture if you prefer or make up in two smaller pans and freeze one.

Serves 8

1 kg lean beef mince

2 onions, chopped

3 fat cloves garlic, chopped

2 420 g cans condensed tomato soup

3 400 g cans chopped tomatoes

2 heaped tsp mixed herbs

1 bay leaf

1½ tbsp butter

1½ tbsp olive oil

4 tbsp plain flour

600 ml low-fat milk

salt and pepper, to season

2 400 g packs fresh lasagne sheets,
    or homemade pasta

2 cups beef stock

¼ cup tomato paste

1 tbsp brown sugar

1 cup loosely packed grated cheese

Preheat the oven to 170°C.

To make the filling, heat a large saucepan and gradually add the mince, stirring continuously until all the meat is used. (You should not need to use any oil.) Stir until browned.

Add the onion and garlic to the pan and cook until soft then mix in the soup and one can of tomatoes, mixed herbs and bay leaf. Simmer for 10–15 minutes.

While the meat sauce is cooking, melt the butter and oil in a medium-sized saucepan and, using a balloon whisk, mix in the flour. Cook the mixture for 1–2 minutes over a gentle heat. Add the milk gradually, whisking thoroughly after each addition to form a lump-free sauce. Simmer gently, stirring with the whisk until the sauce thickens. Season with salt and pepper and set aside.

To assemble the cannelloni, spread a thin layer of the meat sauce over the base of a large roasting tray. Cut the lasagne sheets into 24 strips, place a spoonful of mixture into the pasta and roll up like a tube and place in rows in the tray. Use three-quarters of the meat mixture to fill the tubes — the remainder will become a thin sauce.

Return the remaining meat mixture to the heat, add the remaining 2 cans of tomatoes, beef stock, tomato paste and brown sugar and simmer for 5 minutes. Spoon the thin sauce over the whole pan, easing the sauce in between the tubes and allowing it to work its way around the sides as well. Give the tubes a gentle press to slightly submerge them then spoon over the béchamel sauce. Top with the grated cheese and bake for 40 minutes.

Cook's tip
Buy good-quality mince in bulk when it is on special and freeze in meal-sized lots for later.

Spianata

Spianata is like a rolled pizza, wrapped in delicious, crispy bacon with a generous grating of Parmesan cheese on top.

Serves 6

FOR THE DOUGH
½ cup warm milk
½ cup warm water
1 tsp sugar
1 tbsp dried yeast
½ tsp salt
2 tbsp oil
2 cups plain flour

FOR THE FILLING
2 tbsp tomato paste
1–2 tbsp basil pesto
   (see Cook's tip)
1 bunch baby spinach or
   spinach, washed and tossed
   in a hot pan with 1 clove of
   garlic until wilted (no oil required)
2–3 cups roasted vegetables
   (I usually use pumpkin,
   aubergine and courgette)
grated Parmesan cheese
50 g shaved ham or leftovers,
   such as chicken and pasta sauce
100 g middle bacon
(approximately 3 full rashers)

Preheat the oven to 200°C. Prepare ingredients for the filling.

To make the dough, combine warm milk and water in a small bowl and check the temperature by holding your little finger in the liquid and counting to 10 — it should feel lukewarm. Stir in the sugar and sprinkle yeast on top. After 5–10 minutes it will become frothy. Stir salt and oil into the flour and add yeast mixture. Mix, then knead on a well-floured surface for about 5 minutes. The dough should be smooth and springy by this time. Put it in a greased bowl and microwave 1 minute on low power, stand for 10 minutes then repeat until dough has doubled in size. (Two zaps with the microwave are normally enough.) Roll out to a rectangle 30 cm x 36 cm.

Place the dough on a metal baking sheet and spread thinly with tomato paste and pesto. Spread the spinach and roasted vegetables over the dough, sprinkle with Parmesan cheese and spread the shaved ham or any additional titbits over the vegetables.

Using a spatula, gently roll the dough, enclosing the vegetables. The Spianata should resemble a sponge roll but with the join on the top. Arrange the bacon slices in a criss-cross pattern over the join and sprinkle with Parmesan cheese. Bake for 20 minutes, until golden brown and hollow-sounding when tapped. Serve in thick slices.

Cook's tip

To make your own pesto, mash together a handful of basil leaves, a pinch of salt, a sprinkle of pine nuts, some grated Parmesan cheese and a clove of garlic using a mortar and pestle. Mix together with enough olive oil to form a spreadable paste. In the absence of a mortar and pestle the pesto can be mashed in a bowl using the end of a rolling pin.

I first tried spianata in a café
and became an instant convert . . .

Mushroom and thyme risotto
with roasted chicken and vegetables

This risotto is excellent on its own as a light meal but served with the roasted chicken it becomes a deliciously simple yet stylish dinner for family or guests. The risotto can be made with powdered stock but the dish is best when made with good-quality chicken stock.

Serves 4

FOR THE CHICKEN

1 knob butter

1 splash oil

1 swede, peeled and
  cut into large chunks

1 parsnip, peeled and
  cut into large chunks

1 kumara, peeled and
  cut into large chunks

2 carrots, peeled and
  cut into quarters lengthways

4 little pickling onions,
  peeled but left whole

4 whole chicken legs

FOR THE RISOTTO

1 leek

1 tbsp butter

2 cloves garlic, crushed

3 large flat field mushrooms,
  coarsely chopped

pinch of thyme

1 splash olive oil

¾ cup arborio rice

500 ml good chicken stock

Preheat the oven to 180°.

To cook the chicken, first place the butter and oil into the roasting pan and heat in the oven. Place the prepared vegetables into the pan and toss in the hot buttery oil. Arrange the vegetables in a single layer and place the chicken pieces on top. Roast the chicken and vegetables for 40–50 minutes, until the chicken is cooked and the vegetables are tender and golden.

While the chicken is cooking, prepare the risotto. Trim the leaves and root end from the leek, retaining only the white and pale green portion of the stalk. Cut it in half lengthways and then slice finely. Heat the butter in a large shallow pan and cook the leek and garlic gently until soft but not coloured, add the mushrooms and thyme and allow to soften. Add the oil to the pan, then stir in the arborio rice until thoroughly coated in pan juices. Pour in half the stock, stir well and simmer gently until the stock is absorbed. Add the remainder of the stock little by little, ensuring that it is completely absorbed after each addition. The rice should become tender and the risotto should have a creamy consistency. Add extra stock, if required. Set the risotto aside — if it becomes too thick, add a dash of water, wine or stock to loosen the texture.

When the chicken is cooked and the juices run clear, remove it from the pan and place on a warm plate to rest. Drain off any liquid from the pan, loosen the vegetables and return them to the oven to stay warm while the dish is assembled.

To serve, place a spoonful of risotto on each plate. Nestle a piece of the chicken on top of the risotto and arrange some of the roasted vegetables from the pan on the side.

Cook's tip

Both homemade stock and ready-made liquid stock can be frozen for later. Measure the stock before you freeze it, and write the quantity on the container.

Tasty and packed with loads of lemony zing. Use fresh or dried pasta — whatever you have to hand . . .

Tagliatelle with baby spinach and bacon

Fast and flavour packed, this simple fresh pasta dish is equally good made with dried pasta, such as spaghetti or spaghettini. You can also substitute regular spinach or even silverbeet when baby spinach is not available.

Serves 4

fresh or dried pasta,
   enough for 4 people
2 tbsp olive oil (use lemon-infused
   oil if you have it)
3 rashers good-quality bacon,
   chopped
2 tbsp pine nuts or
   sliced almonds
2 cloves garlic, crushed
several handfuls baby spinach,
   thick stalks removed, trimmed
zest and juice of ½ lemon
grated Parmesan, to garnish

Cook the pasta according to packet instructions.

While the pasta is cooking, heat the oil in a large saucepan. Sauté the bacon until starting to brown, add the nuts and cook with the bacon until toasted. Add the garlic and spinach and toss gently until spinach wilts.

Drain the pasta and add to the pan, tossing to coat the pasta in the bacon and spinach mixture. Add the lemon zest and juice. Taste and adjust lemon accordingly. (I like it quite zingy.)

Pile into bowls and top with grated Parmesan cheese.

FRESH AND FAST

Lean, healthy and full of flavour . . .

Everyone needs a repertoire of dishes that are quick to assemble — or at least quick to cook — and if they are also good enough to serve to guests that's a bonus. I like fast-cooking recipes, not because I'm so importantly busy all the time, but more because I'm actually quite lazy.

Not lazy in the lying on the couch eating chocolates and watching *Oprah* sense (I wish), but show me a recipe with a complicated, time-consuming process or too many ingredients and I just can't be bothered.

That doesn't mean I'll eat any old rubbish either — fast food for me is definitely not synonymous with fried food. I worked hard to get my stomach back inside my body after having the world's biggest baby, so I am conscious of my waistline. It's nice to have one, after all.

These recipes are actually pretty lean and healthy and packed with flavour. I also like the fact that many of them can be cooked on the barbecue — that's a no-go zone for women. Consequently, I can lie back and swill my drink while He does most of the cooking and that suits me very well.

Cajun chicken sandwich with mango salsa

This is one of my favourite meals at the moment. I make up the Cajun seasoning, see page 151, and store it in the pantry to use as required. All I have to do then is prepare the chicken and salsa, toss them into a salad and pile onto the bread for a substantial open sandwich that makes a meal. Another option is to have Him fire up the barbecue and cook the chicken and toast some burger buns. Adding sliced avocado and the mango salsa, He thinks he is a gourmet cook and the family have no idea that what they're eating is actually good for them.

Serves 4

FOR THE SANDWICHES

3 single boneless chicken breasts, skins removed

juice of ½ lemon

1 splash olive oil

3–4 tsp Cajun seasoning

mixed salad leaves (e.g. some iceberg lettuce for scrunch and premixed leaves)

1 avocado, stone removed, peeled and sliced

cherry tomatoes (optional)

1 loaf good crusty bread (the Sciaciatta recipe on page 127 works well for this)

FOR THE SALSA

1 large ripe mango, peeled and diced (chopped, hacked, just get the flesh off the stone)

1 tbsp chopped onion

1 handful chopped coriander

1 tbsp sweet chilli sauce or more, according to taste

1 squeeze lemon juice

Slice the chicken into strips and place in a bowl to marinate with lemon juice, oil and Cajun seasoning for at least half an hour.

Meanwhile make the salsa by placing all the ingredients in a bowl and gently stirring together. Set aside for at least 10 minutes to allow the flavour to develop.

Preheat the oven to 180°C and bake the chicken for 20 minutes, until cooked. Alternatively, cook the chicken on a barbecue, until the juices run clear.

In a large bowl, combine the salad leaves, avocado, tomatoes (if using) and two-thirds of the salsa. Toss lightly then add the cooked chicken. Pile onto toasted bread and top with remaining mango salsa.

Cook's tips

Cajun seasoning can be used with a variety of meats to be grilled or barbecued, as a sprinkle on potato dishes or to season soups and stews.

This dish also makes a great platter salad for buffets, parties and 'bring a plate' events.

Gluten free

Use lightly toasted gluten-free bread for the sandwich, or just enjoy as a salad.

Ribbon noodles with chicken and oyster sauce

While I like all sorts of interesting and exotic Asian-style dishes the family lean more towards the conservative, so I try hard to create a balance that we will all like without it being bland. This simple dish fits the bill perfectly and also works well with beef or seafood instead of chicken.

Serves 4

1 pack dried ribbon noodles,
   enough for 4 people
stock, enough to cook the noodles
2 tsp sesame oil
1 large boneless chicken breast or
   equivalent quantity of other lean
   meat, thinly sliced
2 cups chopped green vegetables,
   such as broccoli, asparagus,
   courgettes and Asian greens
2 tbsp oyster sauce
2½ tbsp soy sauce
½ tsp sugar
1 tsp fresh ginger
1 tsp sweet chilli sauce
extra stock if required

First, prepare the noodles by simmering them in stock (I usually use powdered stock) for around 4 minutes.

Reserve ½ cup of the cooking liquid, drain the noodles, rinse them in cold water to arrest the cooking process and leave them in cold water until required.

Heat the oil in a large pan or wok, add the thinly sliced meat, and toss until cooked, add the vegetables, sauces, seasonings and reserved cooking liquid. Cook until vegetables are tender crisp then add drained noodles to the pan, and extra stock if needed, and heat through. Toss the noodles through the mixture to coat in the flavours and serve when piping hot.

Gluten free
Use rice noodles and check that the stock and sauces are gluten-free.

Honey mustard beef with seasonal greens

This dish is great with rice, but if you are a spud-loving household throw washed and quartered new or baby potatoes into the steamer for a few minutes before you add the rest of the vegetables and serve the whole lot together with the sauce drizzled over the top.

Serves 4

1¼ cups basmati rice
3–4 cups vegetables, such as
    cauliflower, broccoli, asparagus
    and Brussels sprouts
cooking spray
400 g rump steak,
    cut into short batons or strips

FOR THE SAUCE
¼ cup honey
1 tsp butter
1 tbsp wholegrain mustard
1 tsp curry powder
small pinch cayenne pepper

Preheat the grill.

Cook the rice using your usual method. Cut the cauliflower and broccoli into florets, and trim the sprouts, removing outer leaves and incising a cross into the base with a sharp knife. Place a steaming basket over a pot of simmering water, fill with the prepared veg and cover with a tight-fitting lid. Steam until veg are tender crisp.

Heat a frying pan or griddle until very hot, spray lightly with cooking spray and sear the meat quickly in small batches.

To make the sauce, combine all the ingredients in a small saucepan and heat gently.

Place the meat into a heatproof dish, pour over the sauce and place under the grill. Turn the meat frequently in the sauce, cooking to desired 'doneness'. Toss the vegetables in with the meat, coating the veg in the sauce, then pile onto rice on individual plates.

Cook's tip
For instructions on how to boil rice, see page 153.

Honeyed pork and noodle stir-fry

This quick pork stir-fry has an addictive savoury flavour and can be made with any combination of vegetables. Try carrots, broccoli and beans for every day, or asparagus spears and snow peas for a special occasion. When fresh veg is in short supply toss in some frozen veg. If the family are frightened of vegetables serve the stir-fry in small bowls with chopsticks — the kids will be so busy trying to operate their eating utensils they won't think to pick out the 'yucky bits'.

Serves 4

2–3 bundles of noodles
2 tbsp sesame oil
300 g lean pork, thinly sliced
   (pork schnitzel is ideal)
1 onion, chopped
1 tsp grated ginger
1 tbsp soy sauce
2 tbsp honey
2 tbsp sweet chilli sauce
2 tbsp crunchy peanut butter
¾ cup chicken stock
3 cups chopped seasonal
   vegetables

Cook the noodles according to packet directions.

While the noodles are cooking, heat the sesame oil in a wok or large frying pan. Stir-fry the pork then add the onion and ginger and cook for 2–3 minutes until onion is soft.

Add the soy sauce, honey, sweet chilli sauce, peanut butter and stock then toss in the vegetables and mix well, stir-frying until veg are tender crisp.

Divide the noodles between four bowls and pile on the stir-fried pork and vegetables. Spoon over any additional sauce.

Variations
A sprinkle of cashews or crispy noodles makes a tasty addition to this dish.

Cook's tip
Sesame oil not only has a delicious sesame flavour, but it is also heat tolerant and has a low viscosity; in other words it can get very hot without smoking and when heated it thins out so a little goes a long way. This makes it ideal for stir-frying.

If you don't have pork you can use beef or chicken. Sometimes, I even make this using mince — it makes a little go a long way.

Gluten free
Serve with rice instead of noodles.

Orzo salad with chilli basil chicken

Orzo is small rice-shaped pasta. It has a lovely silky texture and is good in soups or salads. This salad, made like a stir-fry, can be eaten hot or cold. For people who don't like seafood, the fish sauce won't make the dish taste fishy — it is there to intensify other flavours in the dish. So, don't leave it out unless you are allergic to it.

Serves 4

1 tbsp sesame oil

1 double boneless chicken breast, thinly sliced

3–4 cloves garlic, crushed

3 spring onions, thinly sliced

1 cup broccoli florets

2 tbsp sweet chilli sauce

½ tbsp fish sauce

½ tbsp dark soy sauce

½ cup chicken stock

1 handful basil leaves

1 handful coriander leaves

juice of ½ lime

1 cup orzo, cooked and drained

extra stock if required

Heat the oil in a wok or frying pan on high heat. Quickly seal the chicken then add the garlic and spring onions and toss so they cook quickly. Add the prepared broccoli and the chilli, fish and soy sauces. Mix through then add the stock. Simmer until the broccoli is tender then toss in the fresh herbs. Add the lime juice. Tip the cooked orzo into the pan, and extra stock if needed, and thoroughly coat in the pan juices. Serve immediately as a warm salad or cool and refrigerate until required.

Gluten free
Use small gluten-free pasta instead of orzo or try using rice.

Satay pork balls

Mince is one of the least expensive cuts of meat, and as it is quick and easy to work with, it is great for those with not much time or culinary experience. This simple flavour combination is savoury and very moreish. The meat mixture can easily be made into patties for the barbecue or grill. It really is very tasty.

Serves 4

FOR THE MEATBALLS
400 g lean pork mince
2 slices of bread, made into
    breadcrumbs
1 clove garlic, crushed
2 spring onions, sliced
1 tsp grated ginger
2 tbsp soy sauce
3 tbsp peanut butter
¼ cup sweet chilli sauce

Preheat oven to 180°C.

To make the meatballs, mix all the ingredients together in a bowl or food processor. Using wet hands, form mixture into balls and bake in a non-stick pan for 20 minutes, shaking the pan during cooking so the balls brown all over. When they are cooked they will be golden brown and crunchy outside and the inside should not be pink.

Serve with salad and warmed pita bread or rice for a change.

Gluten free

Use gluten-free bread to make the breadcrumbs that bind the mixture together, and serve with rice instead of as a sandwich.

Use gluten-free soy sauce.

Madras meatballs

This really tasty spice-combination is very quick to prepare. Baking the meatballs uses less fat than frying and doesn't require constant attention. The meat mixture can also be cooked on the barbecue or shaped into burgers. We usually have the spiced vegetables as an accompaniment, but as a barbecue meal we eat the meatballs with flat bread (cooked on the barbecue), salad and a relish or chutney.

Serves 4–6

1 tbsp oil
1 onion, chopped
1 clove garlic, crushed
½ tsp salt
2 slices fresh bread,
    made into breadcrumbs
1 tsp ground cardamom
½ tsp ground chilli
1 tsp fresh grated ginger
4 whole cloves (the spice
    not the bulb)
½ tbsp curry powder (I use mild
    so the whole family will eat it)
½ tsp ground cumin
cooking spray
450 g lean beef mince

Preheat the oven to 210°C.

Heat the oil in a small saucepan and sauté the onion and garlic until soft. Meanwhile, mix the salt and breadcrumbs into the mince.

When the onion is soft add all the spices to the pan and cook gently for 1–2 minutes, until fragrant, taking care not to burn the spices. Remove from the heat and cool slightly before mixing into the mince. Work the spices into the meat with your hands, then using wet hands form the meat into approximately 28 balls.

Lightly spray a heatproof pan with cooking spray and place the meatballs on the tray, spacing them out to allow heat to circulate. Bake the meatballs for 10–15 minutes. Shake the pan during cooking to brown the meatballs on all sides. When cooked through, remove from the oven and drain on absorbent paper.

Serve 4–5 meatballs with a dollop of natural yoghurt, spiced vegetables, see opposite, and some flat bread.

Gluten free
Use gluten-free bread to make the breadcrumbs.

Spiced vegetables

This is an excellent side dish as it's really quick and easy to prepare. It goes particularly well with dry curries, such as chicken tikka, biryani, meatballs or fish. Don't be put off by the dauntingly long list — they're just spices that are all added at once. The result is aromatic rather than hot.

Serves 4

½ tbsp oil
1 tsp yellow mustard seeds
1 onion, chopped
1 tsp garam masala
1 tsp cumin
1 tsp coriander
1 tsp fresh ginger
1 400 g can chopped tomatoes
1 tsp sugar
1 cup cauliflower florets
1 cup frozen peas or beans
¾ cup chicken stock
1 dsp natural yoghurt
yoghurt and coriander,
    to garnish (optional)

Heat the oil in a medium-sized saucepan and add the mustard seeds. When the seeds are popping add the chopped onion and sauté until soft. Stir in all the other spices and cook gently for 1–2 minutes, taking care that they don't burn. Add the tomatoes, sugar, vegetables and stock and boil for 10–15 minutes, until the vegetables are tender and the liquid is reduced. Stir frequently during cooking.

Remove from the heat and stir in the yoghurt. Serve the spiced vegetables as a side dish.

Cook's tip
Yoghurt must be added last to avoid curdling. First remove the pan from the heat, then gently stir in the yoghurt. Do not allow to simmer once the yoghurt has been added.

Dairy free
Use coconut cream instead of yoghurt.

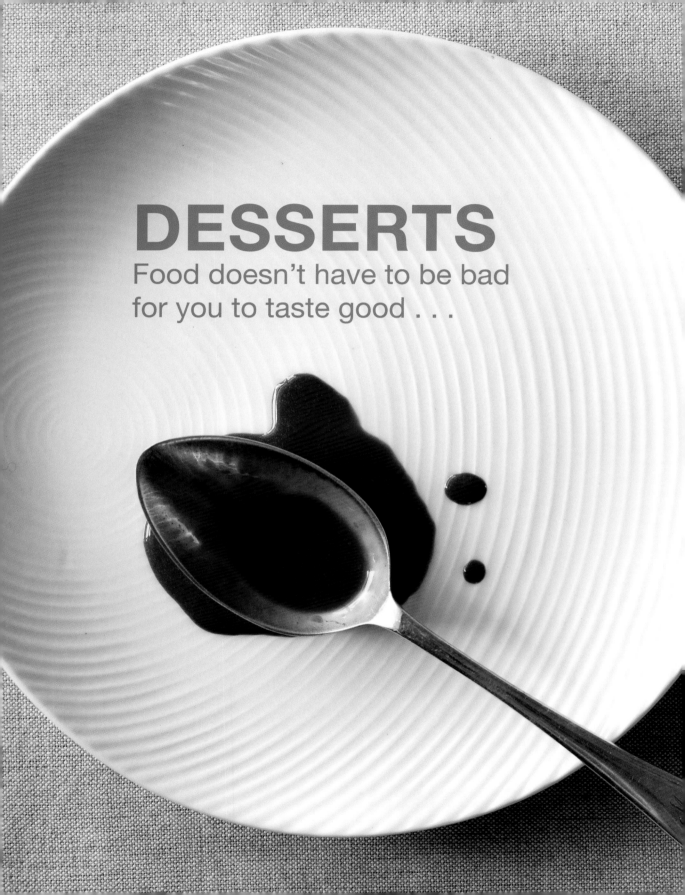

DESSERTS

Food doesn't have to be bad
for you to taste good . . .

I have always thought the best time of the day to enjoy dessert is first thing in the morning, straight from the fridge, off the serving spoon. It's the appetite, you see — after a rich meal I just don't have the appetite to fully appreciate dessert.

It's true — you just have to ask my sister Fran, who can't pass up a scoop or two of cold trifle before her morning chai, given the chance. When we were kids, she inducted me into the mysteries of the pudding-breakfast. While our parents were sleeping off the excesses of a dinner party the night before, we would lose ourselves in an orgy of leftover profiteroles, lemon soufflé, Robert Carrier chocolate mousse or Cordon Bleu rum pie (it was the '70s after all). Then it was back to bed quick smart, and, armed with an apple, a book and a virtuous expression, we'd deny all knowledge — even under torture.

Since those carefree days, we have discovered cholesterol and heart disease, and dessert has become all but a swear word in some quarters. But food doesn't have to be bad for you to taste good — sorbet, gelato, and roasted fruit salad are among my favourite sweet treats and all are remarkably guilt free, though I still hear the faint echo of my mother's voice from the bedroom down the hall shouting 'John, those girls are in the fridge again'.

Caitlin Amelia's rhubarb and almond tart

This dessert is a winner every time. The rich, sweet almond filling contrasts with slightly tart rhubarb in a crispy golden crust. Eleven-year-old Caitlin liked this dessert so much I named it after her and they are both hard to resist!

Serves 4–6

200 g fresh rhubarb
(approx. 3 long stalks)
¼ cup sugar
scant ¼ cup water
50 g butter
⅓ cup caster sugar
½ cup ground almonds
½ tbsp plain flour
¼ tsp vanilla essence
2 eggs
2 sheets ready-rolled puff pastry
1 medium apple, peeled and
sliced thinly
caster sugar, for sprinkling
icing sugar, to dust

Gluten free

Use one quantity of gluten-, dairy- and egg-free sweet pastry, see page 13.

Preheat oven to 200°C.

Trim the ends from the rhubarb and roughly chop the stalks into short lengths. Place in a small saucepan with the sugar and water. Bring to the boil and simmer 7–10 minutes, until the rhubarb is tender and a soft spreadable consistency.

To make the filling, beat the butter until light, add the caster sugar and continue beating until light and fluffy. Stir in the ground almonds, flour, vanilla and 1 egg.

Place a sheet of pastry on a greased baking tray. Brush the edges with water then spread the almond mixture over the pastry leaving a 1-cm border all the way around. Cover the almond mixture with the thinly sliced apple then spread the cooked rhubarb evenly over the top.

Take the second sheet of pastry and roll it with a rolling pin to enlarge it slightly so it can cover the tart and accommodate the filling. Place it over the filling and press the edges firmly to seal. Crimp the edges with the tines of a fork. Make some incisions in the top of the pastry in a decorative pattern, which will allow steam to escape during cooking. Lightly beat the second egg and brush over the pastry, sprinkle with extra caster sugar and bake for 15 minutes, until risen and golden. Dust with icing sugar to serve.

Serve hot or cold with cream, ice-cream or yoghurt.

Dairy free

Use one quantity of gluten-, dairy- and egg-free sweet pastry, see page 13. Use 50 g of a non-dairy substitute instead of butter in the filling.

Lightly grease a baking sheet and roll two-thirds of the pastry into a rectangle approximately 28 cm x 20 cm. Use a spatula or knife to push up the sides a little to form a lip that will prevent the filling running out.

Fill the base with the almond mixture, and then place the slices of apple over the filling. Spread the cooked rhubarb over the top and crumble on remaining pastry. Sprinkle with caster sugar and bake at 200°C for 15–20 minutes, until pastry is biscuit coloured and filling has set. Serve warm or cold.

Bubbly plum pies

This dessert is a good store-cupboard stand-by — a can of plums and a couple of sheets of pastry are all you need. Sugary pastry and piping-hot sweet plums are a pretty irresistible combination and, best of all, it's easy enough for the kids to make. Feel free to use home-bottled plums, if you have some.

Makes 6 single serves

1 400 g can black Doris plums
   (there will be some plums
   left over for another recipe)
2 sheets ready-rolled puff pastry
1 egg
granulated sugar, for sprinkling

Preheat the oven to 200°C.

Drain the plums and remove the stones.

Cut the pastry into 6 circles, rerolling the pastry, as required, to line 6 greased standard muffin cups with pastry. Place a spoonful of plums into each pastry case then roll the pastry out to cut the lids. Brush the edges of the lids with water and press into place.

Lightly whisk the egg and brush over the pies, sprinkle with sugar and bake for 15–20 minutes or until risen, golden and crispy.

Cook's tip
Always make sure the oven is at the correct temperature before cooking pastry — if it is not hot enough when the pastry goes in, the fats in the pastry melt before they have a chance to cook and go crisp, resulting in greasy pastry.

Roasted fruit salad

Warm, sweet, roasted fruit makes a succulent alternative to a traditional fruit salad. Roasting the fruit concentrates the natural sugars so the fruit is deliciously sweet, and the juices combine to form a sublimely exotic (and surprisingly healthy) sauce. Roasted fruit salad is beautiful served warm with ice-cream or mascarpone. Enjoy chilled leftovers on your breakfast cereal or with a dollop of Greek yoghurt, or layer the fruit into a trifle or parfait-style dessert for alcohol-free oomph. (Actually a dash of alcohol, such as rum or Grand Marnier added to the fruit during cooking, is very agreeable, too.)

a selection of fresh seasonal
    fruit, such as peaches, pears,
    nectarines, pineapple, apples
    and apricots (sufficient for the
    number of people to be served)
include 1–2 bananas for
    sweetness, something red
    for colour, such as a couple
    of sliced tamarillos, a handful
    of fresh or frozen berries or
    a few cherries
juice of 1 orange
1 handful brown sugar

Preheat the oven to 180°C.

If using stone fruit, split them and remove the pits. Slice other fruit, such as pineapple, pears or bananas, pick over berries and put all together in a smallish, ceramic ovenproof dish.

Squeeze over the orange juice and sprinkle on the brown sugar and roast in the oven for 10–20 minutes, until fruit is very tender. Serve warm or cold.

Cook's tip

If the dish is too big, all the lovely juices will evaporate — it's better to use a smaller dish and stir the fruit from time to time so it cooks evenly without all the juice drying up.

Mulled-wine baked fruit

The spicy and aromatic flavours of mulled wine fill the house with the scent of Christmas and make ordinary fruit into an exceptionally tasty dessert — best of all, it's pretty healthy too, so make lots!

a selection of fresh seasonal
   fruit, such as peaches, pears,
   nectarines, pineapple, apples
   and apricots
1–2 bananas, for sweetness
something red for colour, such
   as a couple of sliced tamarillos,
   a handful of fresh or frozen
   berries or a few cherries
1 cup red wine
¼ cup orange juice
¼ cup brown sugar
1 cinnamon quill
3 cloves

Preheat the oven to 180°C.

If using stone fruit, split them and remove the pits. Slice other fruit, such as pineapple, pears or bananas, pick over berries (if using) and put all together in a smallish, ceramic ovenproof dish. Bake for 20 minutes.

Combine the wine and orange juice, brown sugar and spices, and pour over the fruit. Bake for an additional 20–30 minutes.

Serve warm or cold with cream, ice-cream, mascarpone, or even meringues. If there is any liquid left after dessert, I suggest you drink it!

Mocha-choc sauce

It's not only for allergy sufferers. This sublime, dairy-free chocolate sauce is excellent for all manner of applications. Drizzle it over puddings, swizzle onto baked bananas with maple syrup, use as a chocolate fondue with fresh fruits, berries and biscotti or eat it straight from the spoon!

Serves 4

1 tbsp dairy-free spread
1 tbsp golden syrup
75 g dairy- and nut-free chocolate
   (preferably with 70 per cent
   cocoa solids)
2 tbsp strong coffee
2 tbsp soy or rice milk
½ tsp vanilla essence

Melt dairy-free spread in a small saucepan, add the golden syrup then remove from the heat and add the chocolate. Stir continuously until chocolate has melted, then stir in the coffee, dairy-free milk and vanilla. Serve warm.

Lemon sorbet

Sorbet — pronounced *sor-bay* — is the ultimate refresher, and an ancient one at that. The simple syrup that forms the basis for sorbet can be made up in advance and stored in the refrigerator. Adding lemon zest to the syrup infuses it with lemon colour as well as extra flavour. The beating part can be done with electric beaters or in a processor.

Serves 8

1½ cups sugar
1½ cups water
2 tbsp lemon zest
1 cup lemon juice (approximately
    5 average–sized lemons)
1 egg white (optional)

Turn the freezer to its coldest setting as the sorbet will need to be removed from the freezer several times to be beaten — a very cold freezer will aid the freezing process.

In a saucepan, combine the sugar, water and zest and bring to the boil, stirring occasionally to ensure all sugar is dissolved. Boil the syrup for 2 minutes then cool.

When the syrup is completely cold, mix in the lemon juice. Taste and adjust the flavour as needed — the mixture should be really lemony and quite sweet as the flavours will dull somewhat once the mixture has been frozen.

Pour into a rigid freezer-proof container and place in the freezer. Remove after an hour or so — the edges should be frozen by this time — and beat with a beater. Return the mixture to the freezer and repeat the beating process several times.

When the sorbet is half frozen, beat the egg white (if using) to soft peaks and fold into the mixture. The frequent beating combined with the concentrated sugar syrup creates the silky smooth mouth-feel that makes sorbet such a delight.

Serve scoops of sorbet in chilled dishes or in a glass topped up with a complementary wine or champagne, as a palate refresher between courses, or in a sugar cone as a low-fat treat.

Cook's tips
Sorbet is best eaten within a few days. However, if it becomes icy, beat with electric beaters or in a processor to restore the consistency.
Egg-free
The egg white makes the texture softer but it is not essential so egg-allergic households can simply omit it.

Boysenberry granita

Granita — pronounced *gran-ee-ta* — is from the same family as sorbet, but has bigger ice crystals. It's like a more sophisticated cousin of the fairground slushy. Yum.

Serves 8

1 cup caster sugar

2 cups water

500 g boysenberries, frozen are
fine (approximately 2½ cups)

juice of 2 lemons (more if required)

Put the sugar and water into a saucepan, heat and stir until the sugar has dissolved then bring to the boil for 2 minutes. Cool the syrup completely and store in the fridge until required.

If using frozen berries, defrost them first then process to a purée and push through a sieve to remove seeds and fibres.

Mix the sieved purée and lemon juice into the cold syrup and taste — use additional lemon juice to add tartness, if required. (Remember the flavours will dull somewhat once the mixture has been frozen.)

Place the mixture into a rigid, freezer-proof container and freeze until edges are crystallised. Use a fork to scrape the crystals into the middle of the container and return to the freezer. Continue the process, scraping the mixture and refreezing three times to produce big irregular crystals.

Serve granita in chilled glasses as a refreshment or dessert accompaniment.

Peach Melba semifreddo

Peaches and raspberries make a sublime combination and this softly frozen — that is what semifreddo means — ice-cream, with its faint tang of yoghurt, is no exception. It's really easy to make and looks gorgeous and tastes even better.

Serves 8

1 410 g can peaches drained,
  to make 1 cup purée (you can
  use fresh peach pulp)
1 cup raspberries, to make
  ½ cup raspberry purée
300 ml cream
150 ml natural, unsweetened yoghurt
½ cup caster sugar
2 egg whites, beaten to soft peaks

Process the peaches to a purée and set aside. Prepare the raspberries. If using frozen berries, defrost them first then process to a purée and push through a sieve to remove the seeds and fibres.

Whip the cream in a large bowl and fold in the yoghurt and caster sugar, peach purée and beaten egg whites.

Lastly, drizzle in the raspberry purée and ripple it through the mixture using the blade of a knife.

Pour the mixture into a clean ice-cream tub, cover with a lid and freeze.

Semifreddo should be softer and creamier than beaten ice-cream. It is lovely in cones, frozen in ice-block moulds or served in bowls with fresh raspberries and a scattering of toasted almonds.

Cook's tip
You can use berry yoghurt instead of natural, but you may need to use less caster sugar — taste the mixture and adjust the sweetness accordingly.

Rich chocolate gelato

Gelato is supposed to be softer than ice-cream and more intensely flavoured. This homemade version is incredibly rich and surprisingly healthy with a softish texture that's pretty hard to resist. It's also egg free, which is great news for people with egg allergies.

Serves 6–8

375 ml trim milk
2 tbsp cornflour
½ cup cocoa
1 375 ml can lite evaporated milk
¾ cup sugar
100 g dark chocolate

Cook's tip
I use Carnation brand lite evaporated milk.

Place 250 ml of the milk in a bowl. Add the cornflour and cocoa and whisk to combine. In a saucepan, combine the remaining milk, evaporated milk, sugar and chocolate and heat gently, stirring until sugar is dissolved and chocolate melted. Pour in the cocoa mixture and stir continuously over a gentle heat for 5–10 minutes, until the mixture is just simmering and has thickened to a pouring custard consistency. Pour the mixture through a sieve into a rigid, freezer-safe container and cover with cling film to prevent a skin forming. When completely cold, freeze until half frozen then remove from the freezer and beat the mixture. Return it to the freezer to freeze completely. The gelato will be best eaten within 3–5 days.

Little tarts

A platter or cake stand piled high with irresistible little morsels is a sweet-lover's fantasy. These pastry cases can be used for any of the following fillings. I bake them in mini-muffin pans.

Makes 24

FOR THE PASTRY
250 g plain flour
110 g butter
110 g caster sugar
pinch of salt
1 tsp vanilla essence
4 egg yolks

Place all the ingredients into the bowl of a food processor and pulse to form a dough or use your fingertips to work all the ingredients into a paste. Knead the dough lightly until smooth. Roll out and cut with a flute-edged cutter.

If the pastry breaks, knead it a little longer and re-roll it: it becomes more flexible with handling. Chill the pastry-lined trays for half an hour in the freezer.

Preheat the oven to 180°C then bake the pastry cases for 10 minutes, until biscuit coloured.

Variations
Fill tart cases with a spoonful of jam or with a spoonful of sharp tangy lemon curd.

Fill tart cases with caramel, see page 90, and top with fresh berries or melted chocolate or toasted nuts or hokey pokey or crushed chocolate coffee beans.

Leave the tart shells empty and offer a selection of fillings for people to make their own flavour combos.

Cook's tip
Use the egg whites to make petit pavlovas, see page 92.

Baby banoffee pies

I adore banoffee pie — the combination of caramel, banana and cream is irresistible. Baby banoffee pies are great for parties — they can be eaten with the fingers and they look and taste sublime. The pastry and filling can be made ahead, allowing for last-minute assembly. This homemade caramel is far superior to ready-made caramel, which always tastes a little cheesy to me.

Makes 24

FOR THE CARAMEL
1 375 g can sweetened
   condensed milk

juice of 1 lemon
3 bananas, sliced
pastry cases (see page 89)
300 ml cream, whipped to
   hold a peak

To make the caramel, remove the label from the tin and completely submerge the unopened can in a large saucepan of water. Boil the can for 2½–3 hours. The condensed milk will turn to golden caramel inside the can.

Squeeze the lemon juice over the banana slices to prevent them browning.

To assemble the pies, fill the prepared pie cases (see recipe page 89) with caramel, pipe or spoon on a dollop of cream and finish by propping a slice of banana on one side of the cream.

Cook's tip

If you are boiling condensed milk tins for 3 hours you may as well do more than one. The extra will keep in the unopened tin in your pantry until required.

Chocolate caramel petit tarts

These irresistible little tarts are completely decadent. Soft caramel, dark chocolate ganache and biscuity pastry make them simply divine! Serve with coffee as an after-dinner treat or with ice-cream for dessert.

Makes 24

pastry cases (see page 89)
½ 375 g can caramel, see above
50 ml cream
50 g dark chocolate

Three-quarters fill each tart case (see recipe page 89) with caramel.

Heat the cream until boiling (I do this in the microwave in a cup). Add the chocolate and stir continuously until chocolate is completely melted. Use a teaspoon to pour chocolate into the top of the tartlets, completely covering caramel. Set aside or refrigerate for several hours until chocolate is set.

Cook's tip

These tarts will keep well in an airtight container for a week.

Pecan fudge pie

Chocolatey and sweet, this pie is great with a cup of coffee or a scoop of ice-cream or both.

Serves 6–8

FOR THE RICH FLAN PASTRY
1½ cups plain flour
75 g butter
3 tbsp sugar
½ tsp vanilla essence
3 egg yolks

FOR THE FILLING
50 g butter
150 g dark chocolate, chopped
1 cup sweetened condensed milk
½ cup brown sugar
2 tbsp cornflour
2 eggs, beaten
1 tsp vanilla essence
½ cup pecan halves
icing sugar, to serve

Preheat the oven to 180°C. Grease a 23 cm loose-bottomed flan tin.

To make the pastry, combine all the ingredients in a bowl or food processor and mix to form a dough. Push the pastry into a ball and wrap in cling film and rest it in the fridge for half an hour before rolling out.

Roll the dough onto a sheet of non-stick baking paper and lift it into the prepared tin. Press the pastry gently into place and neatly trim off the excess. Place the pastry-lined tin into the freezer while you make the filling.

To make the filling, melt the butter in a saucepan and remove from the heat. Add the chocolate, stirring continuously until the chocolate melts. Return to the heat and stir in condensed milk, heating until the mixture bubbles.

In a bowl, whisk together the brown sugar, cornflour, eggs and vanilla. When combined, add to the chocolate mixture and pour into the chilled pie shell.

Decorate with the pecan nuts and bake for 45 minutes, until set. If the pastry is browning too quickly, reduce the temperature to 170°C.

Dust with icing sugar before serving.

Cook's tip
The pie is fudgey and delicious, even without the pecans, so if nuts are an allergy problem, leave them out.

Gluten free
Use 1 quantity of gluten-, dairy- and egg-free pastry, see page 13. Roll the pastry onto a sheet of non-stick baking paper and invert over the tin, gently pressing the pastry into the tin. Peel off the paper and patch and trim the pastry, if required.

Dairy free
Use 50 g of a non-dairy spread instead of butter and use 100 g dairy-free dark chocolate in the filling. Assemble and bake as above. Use dairy-free condensed milk recipe (see page 14).

Petit pavlovas

Pretty individual pavlovas make great party food. This recipe yields a lot of meringues that can be made days ahead and stored in an airtight container.

The secret to meringue is drying it out rather than actually cooking it, so use a low temperature and allow a long resting time in the residual heat once the oven has been turned off. I usually make these in the evening, then they can stay in the oven overnight — two hours' drying time is sufficient, but much less and you are liable to lose a filling or two, as the centres will still be chewy.

Makes 25+ small meringues

4 egg whites
tiny pinch of salt
250 g caster sugar
2 tsp cornflour
1 tsp white vinegar
½ tsp vanilla essence
300 ml cream
3 kiwifruit or other fruit
    for topping, such as
    halved strawberries

Preheat the oven to 160°C.

Splash some water on two baking trays then cover with non-stick baking paper — the water will stop the paper sliding around.

In a large bowl, place the egg whites and salt and beat or whisk until the whites form soft peaks — the mixture should hold its shape without being stiff.

Add the sugar a spoonful at a time, mixing well after each addition. When all the sugar has been added, fold in the cornflour, vinegar and vanilla essence.

Scoop the mixture into a piping bag fitted with a large star nozzle or into a plastic bag with one corner snipped off, and pipe the meringue into smallish mounds, approximately 7-cm diameter. Use a bread and butter knife to scoop a hollow into the middle of each one and place the trays in the oven. Immediately reduce the oven temperature to 140°C and bake the petit pavlovas for 30 minutes — they should have the palest tint of beige to them. If they are browning too much, reduce the oven temperature to 130°C. When cooked, turn the oven off but leave the trays in the oven for two hours or overnight to completely dry out.

To serve, whip the cream to soft peaks and place a small spoonful of cream into the centre of each petit pavlova. Top with a sliver of kiwifruit or a halved strawberry, some passionfruit pulp or berry purée and serve immediately.

Berry shortcakes

This is the kind of dessert I like to make when we have another family over for a casual meal — my kids can help assemble the dish, it looks stunning but is simple, and appeals to a wide age range of diners. You can use slices of strawberry to top the shortcakes if other berries are too pricey, in which case you may like to finish them with a dollop of cream to decorate.

Makes 18 — allow 1–2 per person

FOR THE SHORTCAKES
125 g sugar
350 g flour
pinch of salt
225 g butter

FOR THE TOPPING
½ cup strawberry or raspberry
 jam, warmed and sieved
 to remove seeds
4 punnets fresh berries

Preheat the oven to 150°C.

To make the shortcake bases, combine the sugar, flour and salt in a bowl. Cut the butter into small pieces and rub into the dry ingredients. Work it well with your hands until it becomes a smooth dough or place all the ingredients into a food processor and process until dough forms — you may still need to work it a little with your hands.

Roll the mixture out until it is about as thick as a slice of bread, use an 8-cm diameter cookie cutter or drinking glass to cut 18 circles from the dough, prick each circle several times with a fork. Cook on a greased tray for 20 minutes, until lightly golden. Remove from the tray and cool on a rack.

To assemble the shortcakes, spread a circle of sieved jam into the middle of each shortcake and top with a pile of mixed berries. Arrange on a platter and serve with whipped cream or ice-cream.

Cook's tip

I like to use a mixture of 1 punnet of blueberries, 2 of raspberries and 1 of strawberries — and I halve the strawberries. Brushing with some of the warmed jam will give the berries a glossy sheen.

CELEBRATIONS
Meals that memories are made of . . .

Birthdays and Christmas have always been a big deal in our family — my Mum did these things really well and set the bar pretty high. The baton passed to my sister and I when our Mum died far too young — damned cancer.

While Christmas will never be the same without my ma, our kids love every little bit of our traditions and their birthdays drive them to the very brink of madness with anticipation.

Family traditions give them a framework for expectation and excitement: 'When I go to sleep tonight Mum and Dad will decorate the table with twinkle lights; my presents will be waiting when I wake up; I'll get to use the Celebration Setting at breakfast; the cousins will come for dinner; Grandma will ring from England; we'll have the party; games and cake . . .' They know what is going to happen and they know it's going to be good and they get very, very excited. The framework of their family life is more important to them than the presents and I love that. And it is just a framework, with the details changing from year to year.

It's very hard to replace the sense of belonging that a family celebration conjures up: 'This is our clan, our whanau, and if you are here then you must be pretty important.' But it's never too late to start a new tradition either as traditions are simply things that become more meaningful to you the more times you do them. Food forms an important part of many festivals and traditions, given as gifts, prepared as an offering or — best of all — enjoyed at home with the ones you love. Just add some twinkling lights, and loads of laughter and you have the sort of celebration meal that memories are made of.

Old Dark Beer-baked ham

A cooked ham should be heated through slowly — allow 20 minutes per kilogram for bone-in ham. Glaze is applied towards the end of the cooking time 30–40 minutes before cooking is complete. The Old Dark Beer glaze will generously coat a half ham. Double the quantity if you are preparing a whole ham.

1 cooked half ham on the bone
4–6 fresh bay leaves
whole cloves

FOR THE GLAZE
1 cup of Speight's Old Dark Beer or
    other dark ale
1/3 cup brown sugar
1 heaped tsp wholegrain mustard
zest of 1 orange

Preheat oven to 160°C and calculate the cooking time, as above.

Before cooking, remove the skin from the ham but retain a good thick layer of fat, which looks gorgeous when golden and crispy and will keep the meat moist and flavourful. To pull off the skin, first run your fingers underneath the skin to separate it from the fatty layer underneath. With a sharp knife, score the surface of the fat into diagonal lines then cut through in the other direction to create diamonds. Using whole cloves, stud the bay leaves to the ham in a decorative pattern then press a whole clove into the centre of each diamond. Place the ham in a roasting pan cut-side down to protect the cut side from drying out.

Bake the ham in the preheated oven for the calculated time, adding the glaze (see below) 40 minutes before cooking is completed.

The cut area will bake on the base of the pan, swimming in melted glaze to form a delicious sticky golden crust that everyone will be fighting over.

To make the glaze, combine all the ingredients and, 40 minutes before the completion of cooking, liberally brush the ham with glaze. Repeat the process at regular intervals, sloshing on some of the pan drippings as you go. For a darker glaze, increase the oven temperature to 180°C for the final 10 minutes or so.

Cook's tip
Line the roasting pan with foil before you start and it will be easier to clean.

Left: Old Dark Beer-baked ham and balsamic roasted vegetables with rosemary (see recipe page 100)

Balsamic roasted vegetables with rosemary

This tasty roasted vegetable medley (pictured page 98) has rich rosy colours and a robust flavour, making it a fabulous side dish for any celebration meal.

Serves 8

450 g red-skinned potatoes
450 g golden kumara
450 g peeled pumpkin
2 large parsnips
2 large carrots
2 red onions
3 fat cloves garlic, chopped
¼ cup olive oil
2 tbsp balsamic vinegar
2 large sprigs rosemary
salt, to season

Preheat the oven to 200°C.

Clean the potatoes, but leave the skins on, and cut into 2–2.5-cm cubes. Cut the kumara and pumpkin into slightly larger chunks as they will cook more quickly than the potatoes. Peel the parsnips and carrots, cut in half lengthways, then into quarters lengthways. Cut each strip in half, forming long chunky wedges. Peel the onions, leaving the stalk end intact, and cut into 8 wedges.

Place the prepared vegetables in a large roasting pan and sprinkle on the garlic. Drizzle with oil and balsamic vinegar and toss well before adding the rosemary and a sprinkle of salt.

Roast the vegetables, turning them frequently until golden and tender (approx. 40–50 minutes).

Serve piping hot with roast meats or use in salads, open sandwiches or with couscous as a side dish.

Seriously good cereal

Forget the Weet-Bix on Christmas morning. Prepare this simple cereal the night before. As you sleep or stay up late, the muesli will be absorbing the fruit juice, making it deliciously sweet and tender. Add the decadent tang of fresh berries and yoghurt before serving and you have a show-stopper breakfast without any fuss. It's definitely good enough for a special occasion but easy enough for every day.

FOR EACH SERVING
½ cup good-quality muesli (the nuts
   and grains kind, not flakes
   and rice pops kind)
fresh orange juice
Greek-style yoghurt
berries, fresh or frozen

The night before you need it, spoon the muesli into a tall glass, pour in enough orange juice to just cover the muesli and then refrigerate overnight. In the morning, top with a generous dollop of thick Greek yoghurt and some berries. In the unlikely event that you need added sweetness you can add a swizzle of maple syrup or honey.

Fruit 'n' spice puddings with maple brandy syrup

These puddings look good cooked individually in little ovenproof cups or in Texas muffin pans. Alternatively, bake as one pudding in a 1-litre ovenproof dish.

Serves 6

FOR THE PUDDINGS

75 g soft butter

¾ cup self-raising flour

50 g fresh breadcrumbs
    (1–2 slices of bread, made
    into breadcrumbs)

50 g brown sugar

½ tsp cinnamon

½ tsp mixed spice

1 egg

1 cup fruit mince

½ cup milk (approximately)

FOR THE MAPLE BRANDY SYRUP

¾ cup brown sugar

¼ cup brandy

¼ cup water

Preheat the oven to 180°C. Grease a 1-litre ovenproof dish or 6 individual dessert cups or ramekins.

To make the pudding, rub the butter into the flour and breadcrumbs then mix in the sugar (I do this in the food processor). Add the spices, then make a well in the centre. Combine the egg, fruit mince and milk, and pour into the flour mixture. Stir the dry ingredients into the liquids, adding a little more milk if needed to create a soft dropping consistency. Pour into the prepared dish or spoon into cups. Bake for about 1 hour, until well risen. Individual serves will cook in around half an hour. Serve warm with maple brandy syrup.

To make the syrup, combine all the ingredients in a small saucepan and heat gently until sugar has dissolved. Serve warm with the puddings.

Gluten free
Use 2 slices of gluten-free bread to make the breadcrumbs. Use 1 scant cup of gluten-free flour mix # 2, see page 12, and add 1 tsp of guar gum and 1½ tsp baking powder to the dry ingredients. Combine the dry ingredients then mix in the fat.

Dairy free
Use soy milk instead of cow's milk. Add the liquids to make as smooth a batter as possible. You can do it all in a processor. Lastly, add the fruit mince. Work quickly as the baking powder will start working as the liquid is added.

Merry berry bombes

These pretty, moulded desserts look really flash but are ultra easy to make. The tang of the yoghurt counteracts the sweetness of the meringues so the overall effect is light, creamy and delicious. A few extra berries for garnish won't go astray either for a really smart-looking result.

Serves 8

300 ml cream, whipped to soft peaks
300 ml natural unsweetened yoghurt
12 average-sized meringues or
   8 meringue nests, crushed
2–3 cups fresh or frozen berries or
   a combination
1–2 tsp caster sugar (optional)

In a large bowl, combine the whipped cream, yoghurt and crushed meringues and fold together. Roughly chop 1 cup of the berries and swirl into the mixture, then spoon into ½–¾-cup capacity cups or moulds and freeze.

Place the remainder of the berries in a small saucepan and cook gently until soft and juicy. Add some sugar if it is too tart and set aside until ready to serve.

Remove the bombes from the freezer 5 minutes before you are ready to serve. Dunk each cup into hot water then turn out on a plate, spoon berries over the top and serve.

Gingerbread Christmas trees

Gingerbread is a traditional Christmas treat — I like to make it into Christmas trees, but icing-dipped angels or stars would also look very pretty.

Makes 30 average-sized biscuits

FOR THE BISCUITS
50 ml golden syrup
2 cups plain flour
1 tbsp ground ginger
1 tsp baking soda
125 g butter
½ cup sugar
1 egg yolk

FOR THE ICING
1 heaped cup icing sugar
lemon zest
juice of 1 lemon
dash of water
silver cachous, to decorate

Preheat oven to 180°C.

To make the gingerbread, heat the syrup in a microwave or saucepan until runny. Combine the dry ingredients in a bowl and set aside. Cream the butter and sugar, then add the egg yolk. Mix in the dry ingredients a little at a time, beating after each addition. Lastly, add the warm syrup. Knead the mixture — it will become softer with handling, making it easier to roll. Roll the dough out to 3-mm thickness and use cookie cutters to cut dough into Christmas tree shapes. Re-roll the scraps until all the dough has been used.

Bake for 15 minutes or until golden and cooked. Cool on the trays.

To make the icing, divide the icing sugar evenly between two bowls. Add half of the zest and lemon juice to each, with enough water to make a coating consistency. Making two bowls of icing prevents the icing being spoilt by collecting too many crumbs from the biscuits.

Dip one half of each biscuit into the icing, tilting it forward and back to create a crisp line. Place on a cooling rack with a tray underneath to catch drips. Place a silver ball on each iced point of the tree.

Cook's tip
If the icing is too runny it will be translucent and if it is too thick it becomes difficult to dip the biscuits. I always use two bowls of icing, as it does get a bit crumby.

Gluten and dairy free
Use gluten-free flour mix # 2, see page 12.

Use a non-dairy substitute instead of butter.

The kneading can be done in a processor or beater, as this dough is much softer and easier to work with. Roll the dough between two sheets of non-stick baking paper and cut out shapes. Watch closely during baking to ensure they don't burn.

Make sure icing sugar is gluten free.

Cayle Christmas cake

This recipe is suitable for diabetics. A lot of recipes developed for special diets seem to place all the importance on observing the diet at the expense of flavour, but if a recipe doesn't taste good, then we tend to revert to what we have always eaten and ignore the dieticians' advice altogether. This is particularly true of festive foods. Too often the 'healthy' option is so far removed from our idea of what that food should actually taste like that we'd almost rather go without than eat the substitute.

This is definitely not the case with this Christmas cake — it is rich and dark, but not sticky and cloying. It has a good cakey texture and the nutty spicy flavour of a classic Christmas cake with no added sugar or fat — the sweetness comes entirely from the fruit.

3 cups dried fruit mix (I always pick the green cherries out of the fruit mix because I can't take them seriously)
1 400 g can apricots or peaches, in juice not syrup
1½ tsp mixed spice
¾ tsp cinnamon
zest of 1 orange
½ cup pitted dates
¼ cup cold tea
3 eggs, beaten
⅓ cup sliced almonds
2¼ tsp baking soda
2 cups self-raising flour
16 whole almonds, for decoration
1 tsp melted butter

Preheat the oven to 170°C. Grease and line an 18-cm square cake tin.

Place the dried fruit in a large saucepan and add the juice from the canned fruit, spices and orange zest. Chop the dates and canned fruit into small pieces and add to the pan with the cold tea. Bring to the boil, stirring frequently. Simmer for 1–2 minutes, still stirring, then cool.

When cool add the beaten eggs, sliced almonds, baking soda and flour to the fruit and quickly combine. Stir well to ensure no floury pockets in the mix. Quickly pour into the prepared tin and arrange whole almonds on top. Bake for 1 hour, until dark golden and well risen. A skewer inserted into the cake should come out clean. If the cake browns too quickly place a double layer of paper over the top to protect it.

When cooked, cool for a few minutes in the tin then turn out, carefully remove baking paper and brush the top with melted butter to add a little shine.

Cook's tip
Cut into 40 pieces, each serve contains 15 g carbohydrate.
Gluten free
Use 2 cups gluten-free flour mix # 2, see page 12, and 2 tsp baking powder.
Dairy free
Use a non-dairy substitute instead of butter or omit completely.

All the nutty, spicy flavour of a classic Christmas cake with no added sugar or fat . . .

Sangria

Sangria is a Spanish wine-and-fruit punch, made from whatever fruit is in season and a bottle of plonk. Sangria makes a cheap drop go a long way and is utterly perfect on a hot sticky summer's afternoon.

Vary the ingredients to suit your taste and budget — you can add ¼ cup of brandy, white rum or a complementary fruit liqueur, such as Grand Marnier, or Cointreau if you want more alcoholic kick. Try different fruit juices, such as cranberry or apple. You can use fizzy wine or soft drink if you like a bit of fizz in your drink. The only rules are to let the fruit macerate in the wine overnight and to serve the sangria icy cold from a big jug.

Makes 1.5 litres

750 ml cheap full-bodied red wine
    (1 bottle or measure from a cask)
a selection of fresh fruit
    (I use a nectarine, an orange,
    a lime, a few strawberries . . .)
2 cups orange juice
¼ cup caster sugar
1 cup lemonade (optional)

The night before, slice the fruit (leaving the skin on) and combine the wine and fruit in a large jug. Refrigerate overnight or for at least 6–8 hours to allow the fruit flavours to develop.

Add the orange juice, sugar and lemonade (if using) and taste. Adjust the sweetness to taste by adding a little more sugar, if required.

Sangria can be fizzy or flat, red or white, basic or flash but must always be ice-cold and fruity!

Grand Marnier fraises cooler

This sangria-style punch can be made up the night before or first thing in the morning for an evening event. The lemonade goes in just before you serve.

Makes 1.8 litres or 12 150-ml serves

750 ml cheap full-bodied red wine
    (1 bottle or measure from a cask)
¼ cup Grand Marnier or other
    complementary liqueur,
    such as kirsch (a miniature
    costs about $5.95)
¼ cup caster sugar
1 punnet strawberries, halved
½ orange, sliced with the skin on
2 cups lemonade

Combine the wine, Grand Marnier, sugar, and the prepared fruit in a large jug. Mix well to dissolve the sugar and refrigerate for at least 8 hours or longer to allow fruit flavours to develop. (Overnight works well.)

When ready to serve, add the lemonade and serve ice-cold.

The Celebration Setting

We first heard this idea at a 'hot tips for parents' workshop years ago and have used it ever since. The celebration setting is used to honour everything from a birthday, certificate or achievement to the arrival of an unexpected guest. It enables us to create an event without having to plan a separate meal and it can be used at any time of the day. I'm convinced the morning cereal tastes better when eaten from the celebration plates on a birthday!

One family I know has put together a celebration setting for each of their children: a painted plate, jewelled napkin ring, co-ordinating placemat and a twirly glass. Each setting is stored in its own special bag; the total effect is opulent and very festive and the pieces are precious to their owners. Alternatively, the celebration setting can be as simple as a coloured plate, a stemmed glass and a candle to blow out at the end of the meal. It's the use, rather than items themselves, that makes them special.

Putting together a Celebration Setting

Shop around for special items:

- a beautiful dinner plate
- an unusual glass or goblet — our guys love the twirly wine glasses with the hollow stems so that the drink goes all the way down to the base.
- a placemat
- a special napkin
- a napkin ring is another inexpensive but decorative accessory to add to a sense of occasion
- a candlestick and candles — lighting a candle could be a special privilege and, too, blowing it out at the end of the meal.

No-more-tears cake decorating

These smart and simple cake-decorating ideas are equally handy for anniversaries, adult birthdays and the inevitable work-shout, resulting in a show-stopper of a cake without blood, sweat or tears. Best of all, you won't have to muck around with a piping bag and bits.

Tins: For two or more tiers use a 20-cm cake tin for the base. For the next tier, I have made a small cake tin by cutting down an A10 or catering-sized tin — ask a local café or retirement home if you can have an empty one from their recycling bin. Use a hack saw or tin snips to trim off the top two thirds, and file off rough edges; what remains is a perfect little 15-cm cake tin.

Fresh flowers: Gerberas are funky, bright and last well, white roses and daisies look fine against a chocolate cake but can look 'dirty' against a pale one.

Artificial flowers: These are a good option. Try Spotlight and $2.00 shops.

Edible flowers: You can buy ready-made icing flowers from cake decorating shops.

Another option is to arrange marshmallow slices in an overlapping circle with a dab of icing and a mini m&m in the centre for cute edible flowers.

You can buy ready-made fondant icing in supermarkets and cake decorating shops to colour, roll out and cut into flower shapes.

Lollies: Heaped cascades of jelly beans or Smarties are very effective — the brilliant colours are really attractive and you don't have to worry about the smoothness of the icing underneath. The same goes for chocolate money — just use lots and pile it up. Lollies can also be arranged in easy but funky designs and patterns, such as flowers and swirls.

Ribbon: Check out Spotlight or your local emporium for wired ribbon to wind around a rolling pin to shape into soft coils. If you are using organza ribbon to make a band to go around a cake, allow for a double layer.

Sparkle: Edible glitter and edible paint are easy to apply and go a very long way. Choose a colour that you are likely to use again.

Bought cake: Buy cake a day ahead. Older cake is less likely to shed crumbs through the icing as you spread it.

Candles: Coloured alphabet candles on short spikes are available in $2.00 shops — look for 'happy birthday' or 'I love you'.

Wired stars or hearts: Use florist's wire and ready-made icing to make hearts and stars.

Ready-made fondant dries to a hard, edible finish. I use the Pettinice brand.

Several days ahead, prepare the shapes.

To colour the icing, you can knead the colour through the icing before rolling out or you can cut shapes to paint with edible paints when the shapes are dry.

After the icing has been rolled out, cut stars or hearts from the icing, using a cutter. Wind the pieces of florist's wire around a pencil to make a spring and insert a wire into each icing shape. Leave in the airing cupboard until completely dry and firm.

Poke wires into the cake or cupcakes so the shapes appear to 'spring' out of the top.

Homemade cake: I have adjusted the quantities for these simple and delicious cakes so each will yield an impressive two-tier cake and can made quickly in a grunty food processor if you have one, or in a bowl.

The following recipes make big sturdy cakes that will withstand a bit of handling and are strong enough to support the weight of additional cakes and decorations if you want to stack them up. A food processor or electric beater is recommended.

Lazy daisy cake

One quantity of this mixture makes a big deep 20-cm diameter cake, 1½ times the mixture and you can make a two-tier cake. By doubling the recipe (make two separate batches) you have the right amount of mixture to make a three-tier cake like the one opposite.

FOR THE CAKE

350 g butter

350 g sugar

500 g (3¾ cups) flour

4 tsp baking powder

4 eggs, lightly beaten

2 tbsp lemon juice

FOR THE LEMON FROSTING

200 g butter

3 cups icing sugar

zest and juice of 2 or more lemons

1 additional cup icing sugar

Preheat the oven to 175°C. Grease and line the base and sides of the tin or tins with non-stick baking paper.

To make the cake, beat the butter and sugar in a large bowl until light and fluffy. In a separate bowl, combine the flour and baking powder.

Add the eggs a little at a time to the creamed butter and sugar. Follow each addition of eggs with a scoop of flour, mixing well after each addition until all the eggs and flour are mixed in. Stir in the lemon juice and spoon the mixture into the prepared tin or tins. Scoop a small hollow into the top of the mixture and place in the oven. A 20 cm cake will take approximately 1 hour and 20 minutes to cook — smaller cakes will cook more quickly. A skewer inserted into the centre of the cake should come out clean when the cake is cooked.

Cool the cakes in the tins for 10 minutes before tipping onto a rack.

To make the frosting, beat the butter until pale and fluffy. Sift in the 3 cups of icing sugar a little at a time, beating well after each addition. Add the lemon zest and begin adding juice to taste. Sift in a big spoonful of icing sugar after each addition of juice to keep the texture of the frosting light and fluffy. Continue until the desired lemony flavour is achieved.

To assemble a tiered cake, trim the pointed tops off the cakes and invert — the bottoms are smoother and less inclined to crumb. Stack the cakes, beginning with the largest cake, and insert a wooden skewer through the middle of the cakes to secure the stack. Trim the skewer so that the end is flush with the top of the stack of cakes.

Starting at the top, generously coat the cakes with frosting, working your way down. When the cake is roughly coated, refrigerate to firm the icing up, then smooth the icing using a long metal spatula or palette knife dipped in hot water. It will not be completely smooth but will be pleasingly textured. Refrigerate until firm before decorating with ribbon and flowers. Keep refrigerated until required.

Cook's tip

To make frosting for a three-tier cake use 300 g butter and 4½ cups icing sugar.

Wishing stars birthday cake

This cake looks spectacular with shooting stars springing from the surface of the cake — boys love it! The stars are easy to make, see page 111.

FOR THE CHOCOLATE CAKE
Use Dana's chocolate cake recipe,
   see page 152

FOR THE GANACHE
200 ml cream
200 g dark chocolate

To make the cakes, put all the ingredients into a processor and mix. Pour into the prepared tins. Bake for 50 minutes to 1½ hours, until cakes are risen and springy and a skewer inserted into the cakes comes out clean. (The smaller one will require less time.) Remove from tins and cool on a rack.

To make the ganache, heat the cream until boiling, remove from the heat and stir in the chocolate until melted and refrigerate until it reaches a spreadable consistency.

To assemble the cake, trim the pointed tops of the cakes and invert, the bottoms are smoother and less inclined to crumb. Place the smaller cake on top of the bigger one and generously coat with ganache, starting at the top and working your way down. Smooth as you go using a long metal spatula or palette knife. It will not be completely smooth but will be pleasingly textured. Refrigerate until firm before decorating with ribbon, candles and spike stars into the centre of the cake.

Cook's tip
I use Cadbury Belgian-style chocolate for the ganache.

Hard-out chocolate curlz cake

One tier looks best for this cake, so use 1 quantity of Dana's chocolate cake recipe (see page 152) and the ganache recipe above. Trim the cake when cooled and turn upside-down before decorating.

TO MAKE CHOCOLATE CURLZ
1 sheet of clear plastic acetate or
   overhead projector film
   (from a stationery shop)
½ cup chocolate melts

Melt ½ cup of dark or white chocolate melts over a low heat or in the microwave on low. Use a metal spatula to spread the melted chocolate in a thin, even layer over the plastic film. Hold in the open freezer until the surface begins to set then score the chocolate with a knife in wiggly lines. When dry to the touch but not fully set roll the film quite snugly from corner to corner and secure with a rubber band. Refrigerate until fully set. Remove the band, peel off the curlz and arrange on top of the cake. Dust with a little icing sugar, if desired.

Gluten- and dairy-free party food for kids

If your children or their friends have food allergies, you know that it's the 'being different' that makes the going tough sometimes, but it doesn't have to be like that all the time. Parties are for special treats and there are plenty of treats you can provide for kids with allergies.

Popcorn: Melt honey and pour over freshly popped corn or dust with icing sugar.

Plain potato chips: Check the ingredients to ensure they don't contain dairy solids — even potato chips can have dairy products in them!

Sushi: It's hard to believe but kids love sushi, so make plenty but keep it plain using chicken or fish, and skip the wasabi.

Birthday cake: I use Dana's gluten- and dairy-free chocolate cake, see page 152, decorated with lollies.

Fruit and lolly kebabs: Use bamboo skewers and alternate chunks of fruit, such as banana, strawberries, grapes and pineapple with lollies, such as jelly beans, wine gums, jet planes, natural confectionary company jellies or other allergy-safe sweets. Cadburys produce a comprehensive range of gluten-free products that are listed on their website. However, many of them contain dairy products, so careful checking of all commercially manufactured products is required. Be aware that bags of mixed sweets may have been contaminated — choose carefully.

Jellies: Add chopped fresh fruit and allergy-safe lollies as the jelly begins to set so the treats are suspended in the jelly.

Allergy-safe cookies: Buy or make plain allergy-safe cookies and ice with glacé icing, see page 136. Decorate with sprinkles.

Dairy- and egg-free cupcakes: see page 136.

Chocolate dipped strawberries: see page 138.

Individual pizzas: Make small bases with basic dough, see page 12, and offer a selection of toppings in small bowls. Put a sheet of non-stick baking paper on a metal tray, arrange the bases on the sheet and write each child's name next to their personalised pizza, so they know which one is theirs, when they come out of the oven. If you are including ingredients that may be allergy triggers be very careful to avoid contaminating the rest of the food. Be aware that processed meats, such as ham and salami, may contain traces of gluten.

BAKING

The everyday stuff that makes a house smell like a home . . .

Moaning about my terrible kitchen has become something of a hobby for me. Both of the houses we have lived in since we married have had diabolical kitchens, and significant renovation has never really been an option. We've also become a repository for other peoples'

cast-off kitchen bits — second-hand ovens, third-hand dishwashers, and a prehistoric microwave, all of which have provided me with ample material for my moaning.

However, the day is drawing near when I will no longer have an oven that vents scalding steam onto my stomach. Luxury: a hob with elements that will simmer rather than scorch and, best of all, I'll be freed from the unrelenting heat of a skylight directly over the workspace. It will be goodbye to the 80s wooden bench tops and hip-hooray to sleek, modern lines.

As I write this, however, I can't help thinking about a pioneer bride called Sarah Higgins, who in the 1850s wrote that she was pretty sick of her kitchen, too: 'Now, I wanted a good kitchen but my husband could not leave his work to do it. He helped me to mix the clay before he went to work then I got a little maid to mind the children, while I put up a mud kitchen, 20 ft long and 12 ft wide. The men did the chimney and made a mud oven to bake our bread in.'

It's pretty humbling really. Sarah would have thought my kitchen the height of luxury being that it's not made of mud, and my oven manages to bake the bread well enough despite its many shortcomings, and not just bread but crackers, biscuits, muffins and muesli bars — the everyday stuff that makes the house smell like home when the kids come tumbling through the door after school. Baking that can be tucked into a lunchbox or picnic basket, scoffed for a snack or whipped up in a rush — even a really basic oven like mine can manage that, too. As for Sarah's made-from-mud bread-oven — it would be the height of culinary fashion these days, if only she knew!

Gluten-free Italian herb bread

Tasting similar to herby foccacia bread, this is great for dunking in soups, taking to picnics or toasting to make bruschetta.

2½ cups gluten-free flour
   mix # 1 (see page 12)
1½ sachets dried yeast
½ tsp salt
1 tsp sugar
2 tsp Italian seasoning,
   see page 151
1 tbsp oil
2 tsp guar gum
½ cup warm milk
½ tsp wine or cider vinegar
   (don't use malt vinegar)
3 eggs

In a bowl, combine the flour, yeast, salt, sugar, seasoning, oil and guar gum.

Warm the milk, add the vinegar and eggs, and beat thoroughly. Mix into the dry ingredients and knead with the mixer for 2 or 3 minutes until the mixture is smooth and elastic.

Place the bowl inside a clean plastic bag or cover with cling film and place in the microwave on low power (10 per cent) for 1 minute. Let the dough rest for 20 minutes then tip into a well-greased, round, 20-cm, loose-bottomed flan tin. Using a piece of non-stick baking paper, gently press the dough into the tin, trying not to knock all the air out of it.

The dough needs to double in size in the tin before you bake it. You can cover the dough with plastic and leave in a warm place for 50 minutes or until doubled but I find the dough rises more quickly in a warm, not hot, oven — turned off so the dough rises but doesn't cook (I warm the oven while the dough is resting in the bowl, then turn it off).

When the dough has nearly doubled in size, preheat the oven to 190°C — removing the rising loaf first. When the dough has doubled its original size bake, the loaf for 20 minutes, until pale golden. It will be lighter in colour than a wheat loaf and it will sound hollow when tapped on the bottom. Cool on a wire rack. Serve in wedges or long slices. It's great for dunking.

Clockwise, from left: Rosemary sciaciatta (recipe page 127); gluten-free plain white loaf (recipe page 12); and gluten-free Italian herb bread

Breakfast brioche

Brioche is a French bun made from deliciously cakey, enriched dough. This simplified recipe yields 12 generous brioches for a real café-style snack. The chocolate and berry centre is optional.

Makes 12

1 cup warm milk
1/3 cup plus 1 tsp sugar
1½ tbsp active dried yeast granules
¾ tsp salt
4 cups high-grade flour
110 g butter, melted
4 eggs (one is for glazing)
100 g or 12 squares good dark chocolate
1 cup berries (if using frozen, defrost first)

Place ¼ cup of the warm milk in a small bowl; add the teaspoon of sugar and sprinkle on the yeast. Set aside to turn frothy.

In a large bowl, combine the remaining ¾ cup milk with 1/3 cup sugar and the salt. When the yeast mixture is frothy, add it to the milk mixture in the large bowl.

Use a wooden spoon to beat in 1½ cups of the flour and all the butter. Mix until smooth then use a rubber scraper to gather the mixture, which should resemble a thick batter, into a mound in the middle of the bowl. Cover with a tea towel and set aside in a warm place (or use microwave method, page 127) for around 40 minutes or until doubled in size.

When the mixture has doubled, beat 3 of the eggs and add them to the mixture a little at a time, mixing well after each addition. Beat in two more cups of flour — if you have a kitchen appliance grunty enough to do this, use it! Otherwise, use the wooden spoon and a little creativity to incorporate the flour. Begin kneading the mixture into a ball while in the bowl. (If the mixture is too soft or 'slack' to knead, add some of the remaining flour.) Sprinkle flour onto the bench and knead on the bench for 2–3 minutes until the dough is smooth and satiny and not sticky — you may need to dust with flour while kneading.

Grease a 12-cup muffin pan and divide the dough into 12 equal pieces. Cut one-quarter off each of the portions of dough so you have 12 big blobs and 12 little blobs. Press the larger pieces into the muffin pans; place a piece of chocolate and ½ tsp of berries into the middle of each one. Pull the dough around the filling, pinching the dough to enclose it completely. Roll the smaller pieces into balls and place one on top of each filled brioche. Set aside to rise for 20–30 minutes.

Preheat the oven to 180°C.

When dough is doubled in size, beat remaining egg and brush over the brioches then bake until dark golden and glossy. Serve warm or split in half and toast under the grill until crispy.

Cracker snaps

Crackers are a great snack food, having no sugar and only a little salt. Put them in the lunchbox with a little pot of dip, serve as after-school snacks or make them for your next cheese board.

Serves 4

1 cup plain flour (I often use half
   plain and half wholemeal)
½ tsp salt
2 tbsp butter
2 tbsp sesame seeds, poppy seeds
   or a combination
¼ cup water

Preheat the oven to 200°C.

Place the flour, salt, butter and seeds in a bowl or food processor. Mix well then add the water to form a soft dough.

Roll the dough on a floured bench to desired thickness, prick with a fork and cut into pieces. (I use a zig-zag pasta cutter for crinkled edges). Place the crackers on a floured tray and bake for 15–25 minutes until golden. When cool, snap the crackers apart, if necessary, and serve.

Make whatever shape or size you like, add different varieties of flour, herbs, nuts, seeds, spices and/or cheese to vary the basic cracker.

Gluten and dairy free

While different from the wheat flour version, which doesn't require much in the way of seasoning, these crackers are good and crisp, sturdy enough for dipping into hummus or other dips, and the savoury seasoning means they can be eaten as is. Use 1 cup of gluten-free flour mix # 2, see page 12. Do not add guar gum. Use Olivani or some other non-dairy spread instead of butter. Add ½ tsp Mexican seasoning, see page 151. The seasoning masks the flavour of the flour and gives the crackers a moreish savoury taste. If dairy is not an allergy problem, add some Parmesan cheese.

Mix with water according to the recipe and roll the dough out between two sheets of non-stick baking paper. Cut into shapes and prick with a fork. Sprinkle with salt (I use sea salt) and bake on a greased tray for 15–25 minutes until the crackers are crisp.

From left: Nicholson oat cakes
and cracker snaps

Nicholson oat cakes

Oat cakes are my dad's favourite, spread with butter or served with cheese.
They are salty, savoury and Scottish in origin. Great for cheese boards, or to
make as a gift for a cheese-lover.

360 g oatmeal
100 g plain flour
2½ tsp salt
1 tsp baking powder
2 tbsp sugar
130 g butter
200 ml milk

Preheat oven to 200°C.

Combine all dry ingredients, add the milk and mix for several minutes.
This is best done in a food processor.

Roll out very thin and cut into biscuits. Bake 15–20 minutes.

Muesli-bar magician

Some years ago, I published a recipe for binding muesli together to form bars. The original recipe produced inconsistent results, but I still thought it was a great idea so I've come up with a new formula to turn any muesli into bars.

I have tested it on posh muesli with lots of nuts and exotic fruit, cheap basic muesli and low-fat — lots of rice pops in it — type muesli and they were all successful.

Makes 18 big bars

200 g butter
5 tbsp golden syrup
5 cups muesli
1½ cups plain flour
½ cup sugar
1 tbsp baking soda
¼ cup boiling water

Preheat the oven to 180°C. Grease a 33 cm x 24 cm sponge roll tin.

Melt the butter and golden syrup together in a saucepan or microwave. Combine the muesli, flour and sugar in a large bowl. Dissolve the baking soda in the boiling water and add to the butter and syrup. Pour the liquid into the muesli mixture and mix thoroughly.

Using wet hands, press the mixture into prepared tin and roll firmly over the top with a can or jar to compress the mixture. Run a knife around the edges of the tray to neaten and firm the edges. Bake for 12 minutes, until golden and firm.

Cool in the tray before slicing.

Cook's tip
I have tried many times now to make this with commercially produced gluten-free muesli but the results have been too horrible to contemplate. Rest assured that if I succeed in creating a gluten-free master mix that works, I'll let you know.
Dairy free
Use a non-dairy substitute instead of butter.

From left: Muesli-bar magican and any-berry buckle (see recipe page 126)

Any-berry buckle

People often tell me they simply don't have time to bake but I can't imagine a home without fresh baking. A handful of recipes that are simple to assemble, can be served a variety of ways, and made with whatever you have to hand make it possible for everybody to enjoy homemade baking. This recipe fits the bill.

FOR THE BASE
175 g butter
150 g caster sugar
½ tsp vanilla essence
3 eggs
375 g self-raising flour
pinch of salt
dash of milk

FOR THE TOPPING
1–2 cups fresh or frozen berries or
    sliced fresh fruit, such as apricots,
    peaches or plums
sugar, for sprinkling
icing sugar, for dusting

Preheat the oven to 190°C. Grease a 33 cm x 24 cm sponge roll tin.

Cream the butter and sugar until pale and light, add the vanilla and beat in the eggs one at a time. (I do all this bit in the food processor.)

Fold in the flour and salt and add a dash of milk, then spread the batter into prepared tin.

Scatter the fruit over the top, sprinkle with sugar and bake for 20 minutes, until golden, risen and set in the middle. Dust with icing sugar before serving.

Serve warm or cold as a slice or for dessert.

Cook's tip
Buckle makes a very acceptable dessert, served with cream, Greek yoghurt or a scoop of dairy-free ice-cream or yoghurt.

Gluten and dairy free
Use 375 g or 2¾ cups gluten-free flour mix # 1, see page 12, 3 tsp baking powder and 3 tsp guar gum.

Use a non-dairy substitute instead of butter and a dash of soy or rice milk instead of cow's milk.

The mixture is less of a batter and more of a dough so spread it using a sheet of non-stick baking paper and invert over the prepared tin.

Dust with gluten-free icing sugar before serving.

Rosemary sciaciatta

Sciaciatta, pictured on page 118, is a flat bread from Italy that is pressed down with the fingers to create air holes in the bread, making it great for dunking. Serve it warm, cut into strips with a selection of dips, olives, cheeses or whatever else takes your fancy.

Makes 2 big loaves or 4 smaller loaves

1 tsp sugar
½ cup warm water
1 tbsp dried yeast
6 cups plain flour
2 tsp salt
2 tbsp rosemary, chopped
2 tbsp olive oil
2 cups warm water
extra flour, to dust
¼ cup olive oil
2 tbsp coarse salt
1 handful of small rosemary sprigs

In a small bowl, dissolve the sugar in the first quantity of warm water, sprinkle on the yeast and set aside until frothy.

In a large bowl combine the flour, salt, chopped rosemary and oil.

When the yeast mixture is frothy, add to the flour and stir in, along with the 2 cups of warm water. Mix to form a dough then knead on a floured bench for 5 minutes, until smooth, springy and elastic. Dust the dough with flour, as required, during kneading. Place the dough into a clean greased bowl and cover with greased cling film. Place the dough in a microwave and heat on low power for 1 minute, rest for 10 minutes then repeat, until dough has doubled in size.

Preheat the oven to 200°C. Turn dough onto the floured bench and punch the dough down, kneading lightly. Divide into two pieces. Roll and stretch the dough into two large oblongs and transfer to baking sheets. Brush with olive oil, sprinkle with coarse salt and scatter with small rosemary sprigs. Using fingertips, press dough to create dimples all over the surface of the loaves. Bake in the preheated oven for 20–30 minutes, until golden and loaves sound hollow when tapped. Cut into strips and serve with dips or soup.

Wholemeal lemon and poppy seed cake

Really easy cakes like this are a blessing.

FOR THE CAKE

200 g butter

1 cup sugar

3 eggs

1 tsp vanilla essence

⅓ cup lemon juice and
   lemon zest

1¼ cups wholemeal flour

1¼ cups plain flour

3 tsp baking powder

1 tbsp poppy seeds

½ cup milk

FOR THE LEMON SYRUP

¼ cup lemon juice and zest

¼ cup sugar

Preheat oven to 180°C. Grease and line the base and sides of a 24-cm diameter, loose-bottomed cake tin.

Cream the butter and sugar. Add eggs, vanilla, lemon juice and zest and fold in the dry ingredients, poppy seeds and milk. Pour the batter into the prepared tin and bake for 45 minutes or until the cake is risen, springy and deliciously golden. Remove from the oven and while still warm, drizzle the syrup over the cake.

To make the syrup, heat the lemon juice and zest and sugar in a small pan, stirring until sugar is dissolved.

Serve warm or cold.

Gluten- and dairy-free chocolate pecan crunchies

I haven't made a wheat-flour version of these biscuits, as I like them just as they are. They're a good crunchy cookie to have with a cup of coffee or as a snack.

110 g non-dairy butter substitute

¼ cup sugar

1 tbsp golden syrup

1 tsp vanilla essence

1 cup gluten-free flour mix # 2
   (see page 12)

1 tsp baking powder

¼ cup chopped pecan nuts

¼ cup dairy-free chocolate chips or
   chocolate chopped into chunks

Preheat the oven to 160°C. Line a baking tray with non-stick baking paper.

Cream the fat and sugar, add syrup, vanilla, baking mix and baking powder then fold in the nuts and chocolate chips. Roll into balls and place on prepared tray. Press lightly with a fork to flatten and bake for 15 minutes, until golden. Cool on a rack.

Mars Bar slice

My sister's friend Leanne used to make this slice when the kids were littlies and our three families all holidayed together. I have two kids, my sister has four and Leanne has five. Our combined 11 children included a set of identical twins, a child with ADHD, one diabetic and one with Asperger's syndrome.

You can imagine how happy the adults were at the end of each day when we had all the kids in bed and the Mars Bar slice could come out of hiding.

Makes 24 serves

75 g butter

3 60 g Mars Bars, cut in small pieces

5 cups Ricies or similar

270 g Cadbury Belgian-style
   chocolate or other good
   dark chocolate

Line a 33 cm x 24 cm swiss roll tin with non-stick baking paper.

In a large saucepan, gently melt the butter and chopped-up Mars Bars, stirring constantly until completely melted.

Using a large spoon, fold in the Ricies, mixing thoroughly, and tip into the prepared tin. Use a spatula to press the mixture in firmly, ensuring it is well compacted, especially around the edges.

Melt the chocolate in a bowl over a small saucepan of hot water. Spread with a spatula over the slice and refrigerate until set.

Cut into pieces and serve after the kids have gone to bed.

Gluten- and dairy-free brownie

My family think this gluten- and dairy-free version of my popular chocolate brownie is, frankly, jaw-droppingly good. You could double the recipe and make it in a swiss roll tin but dairy-free chocolate is expensive compared with chocolate that contains milk solids. Nine pieces is a good yield for the cost of the ingredients, but make more if you can afford it.

Makes 9 squares

110 g non-dairy butter substitute

1 cup sugar

100 g good-quality dark
   dairy-free chocolate

¼ cup good-quality cocoa

2 eggs

¾ cup gluten-free flour mix # 1
   (see page 12)

1 tsp guar gum

1 tsp vanilla essence

Preheat the oven to 180°C. Grease an 18-cm square tin and line with baking paper.

Melt butter substitute, remove from the heat and stir in sugar and then chocolate. When the chocolate has melted add the cocoa and eggs, beating thoroughly to combine. Stir in the flour, guar gum and vanilla. Mix well then pour into the prepared tin.

Bake for 25–35 minutes, until firm but still fudgey — good brownie is papery on top and fudgey in the middle.

Caramello brownie

Easy to make, and awfully good. Lovers of the chocolate–caramel combo will go weak at the knees. Serve cold as a sweet treat or warmed with ice-cream as an after-dinner delight.

Makes 24 pieces

FOR THE BASE
150 g butter
1½ cups sugar
150 g dark chocolate
1 tsp vanilla essence
3 eggs
¾ cup flour
¼ cup cocoa

FOR THE CARAMEL
55 g butter
¾ cup condensed milk
1 tbsp golden syrup

Preheat oven to 180°C. Line a 33 cm x 24 cm swiss roll tin with non-stick baking paper.

In a medium-sized saucepan, melt the butter. Stir in the sugar then remove from the heat and add the chocolate and vanilla. Beat in the eggs one at a time then sift in the flour and cocoa, mixing well after each addition.

To make the caramel, melt the butter with the condensed milk and syrup in a small saucepan. When melted and combined remove from the heat and pour into a jug.

Pour some of the chocolate mixture into the prepared tin then alternately pour in some of the caramel mixture, so the two are randomly spread about the tin. Use a meat skewer to swirl the caramel into the chocolate mix.

Bake for 30 minutes, until a knife inserted into the cake comes out clean and the texture is slightly fudgey. Allow to cool before cutting.

Flapjack

Not to be confused with fat breakfast pancakes, this flapjack is a Scottish slice made with oats that is incredibly simple to make.

Oats are very nutritious and flapjack keeps well. It's perfect with a mug of tea or glass of milk and you might like to try it crumbled over ice-cream as a crunchy topping.

Makes 24 pieces

175 g butter
$\frac{1}{3}$ cup golden syrup
150 g brown sugar
400 g medium-sized porridge oats

Preheat the oven to 180°C. Line a 33 cm x 24 cm swiss roll tin with non-stick baking paper

Melt together the butter, golden syrup and brown sugar and mix in the oats.

Press into the prepared tin and compact the mixture, pressing down firmly with a spatula or palette knife.

Bake for approximately 20 minutes, until golden brown. Remove from the oven and score into pieces with a sharp knife. Cool completely before removing from the tin. Store in an airtight container.

Cook's tip

Opinion is divided regarding oats and allergies — some people prefer to avoid them on the basis that, even though they don't contain gluten, they may be contaminated. If that is not a problem for you, flapjack will be an excellent addition to your gluten-free repertoire.

SWEET DREAMS

I have a long-standing love of icingy things . .

One afternoon a while back, I discovered that my son Jack and one of his little friends had devoured a whole tin of cupcakes at one sitting. In fact, they had simply eaten the sugary icing tops off every one, and then biffed the boring remainder into the garden. I found it very hard to be cross as they had simply done something that I have only dreamed of doing.

I have a long-standing love of icingy things, and have been known to drive long distances for a particular French pastry with icing so

tooth shatteringly sweet that I get the shakes after eating a whole one. Bliss. I even like the junk cake they sell in the supermarkets provided it has pink icing on it. God help me if I ever get diabetes.

I have always liked little individual serves — I'm a complete sucker for anything in miniature. I love those dinky little bottles of wine you get on aeroplanes, and dolls' house crockery and Barbie shoes and quails — sooo cute, and those little individual cakes in cafés all garnished and glossy that require you to have a whole one all to yourself.

Not only do I like to eat sweet stuff, I enjoy making it and homemade goodies are accepted currency in most social situations. Turn up unannounced but armed with something sweet that you whipped up earlier and you are virtually guaranteed a warm welcome anywhere. If that doesn't happen, pop round to my place, but make sure you bring the goodies with you.

Egg- and dairy-free cupcakes

A party just wouldn't be a party for my kids if there weren't any cupcakes. Last year, I adapted my regular cupcake recipe to accommodate Jack's mate Isaac's dairy and egg allergies and none of the kids at Jack's birthday appeared to notice any difference. Simply put, they scoffed the lot.

Get the kids to slosh on the icing with plenty of sprinkles or a lolly on the top and they'll be happy.

Makes 24 cupcakes

1½ cups self-raising flour
1 tsp baking powder
½ cup sugar
pinch of salt
50 g non-dairy fat
1 cup soy or rice milk
1 tsp vanilla essence

GLACÉ ICING
1 cup icing sugar
squeeze of lemon juice or
    a drop or two of artificial
    colour and flavour, such
    as raspberry or peppermint

Preheat the oven to 190°C — not fan bake.

Spray mini-muffin pans with non-stick baking spray or line with paper patty cases.

Sift the dry ingredients into a bowl. Melt the non-dairy fat, add the milk and vanilla and fold into the dry ingredients.

Bake for 10–15 minutes until golden. When cool ice with glacé icing.

To make the icing, combine all the ingredients, using only as much water as you need to make a spreadable icing. Ice the top of each cupcake with icing and decorate as desired.

Cook's tips

The structure of the batter is very fragile and when baked using the fan setting on my oven the little cakes rise like the Leaning Tower of Pisa — at all sorts of funny angles.

I have tried making these egg-, dairy- and gluten-free, but without either egg or gluten there is nothing to support the mixture and hold it up — the end result was pretty nasty.

Left: Egg- and dairy-free cupcakes; lemony snickets (see page 138)

Lemony snickets

These pretty lemony lamington-style cakes (pictured on page 137) are dead easy to make and look divine sprinkled with silver cachous and garnished with a strawberry or two. Keep a supermarket trifle sponge in the freezer, then when you need a plate of cake in a hurry, you can throw these together.

Makes 36

1 trifle sponge, preferably
   one day old
1 cup thread coconut
3 cups desiccated coconut
runny icing made from
   icing sugar, plenty of
   lemon juice and a little water

Peel or slice off the brown outer layer of the sponge so you are left with the yellowish cake, and cut into 36 squares. Combine the coconut threads and desiccated coconut in a large bowl.

Dip a square of sponge first in the icing, submerging it quickly with a fork then whipping it out before it sucks up a gallon of icing and drop it in the coconut. When you have dipped 3 or 4 pieces of sponge, toss them around gently in the coconut and set them aside on a platter for the icing to harden. Continue until all the squares are dipped and dunked. When they have firmed up a little, pile them up and sprinkle with silver balls and halved strawberries.

Chocolate-dipped strawberries

Simple, delicious and gorgeous to look at, this summer treat is too good to ignore and, with careful selection of the chocolate, it can be allergy safe, too.

Good-quality dark chocolate
   (dairy-free, if necessary)
ripe strawberries cleaned and
   dry but with the stalks intact

Place a heatproof bowl over a small saucepan of simmering water. Break the chocolate into the bowl and remove from the heat. Allow the residual heat to gently melt the chocolate. Dip each strawberry three-quarters of the way into the melted chocolate. Allow the excess chocolate to drip off, then place on the baking paper and refrigerate until set. These are best eaten the day they are made.

Cook's tip

Chocolate will melt in the palm of your hand. In fact, if it gets too warm instead of melting it seizes and becomes stiff and horrible. Don't be impatient and try to speed up melting chocolate or you are likely to ruin it.

Chocolate melts and similar products can be heated by microwaving because they are made from vegetable fat not cocoa butter, but that is reflected in the flavour. Use the best quality chocolate you can afford and think of all the wonderful health benefits to be gained from the antioxidants — not to mention the sheer joy of consuming good dark chocolate.

Sweetie treatie tree

The table decoration is fun and easy to make — it can be used as a gift as well as reused at home year after year.

enough plaster of Paris to fill the
    pot and secure the stick in place
1 small terracotta pot
1 sturdy stick or piece of dowel
1 polystyrene ball
double-sided sticky tape
wrapped sweets and treats, such as
    chocolates, mini Mars Bars or
    similar, candy canes, truffles,
    bags of m&m's, etc.

Make up the plaster of Paris according to the packet instructions and pour into the pot. (You may need to plug up the drainage hole in the bottom of the pot.)

Insert the stick into the centre of the plaster and leave to set. When completely dry, whittle a hole into the polystyrene ball so that it fits snugly and securely onto the stick.

Cut strips of double-sided sticky tape and wrap all over the ball. Press individually wrapped treats onto the ball until it is completely covered.

Take the sweetie treatie tree as a gift or after-dinner treat for friends, use at birthday parties or as a table centrepiece.

To reuse, remove old sticky tape and replace with fresh tape and a new stock of goodies. Our sweetie treatie tree has given more than 10 years' service and is still going strong.

Sherbet

This good old classic requires no heating so it's a safe sweetie for younger cooks to make. The recipe has been used in our family for years. Sherbet is great sprinkled on ice-cream, sucked through a straw or licked from a spoon.

1 tsp citric acid
1 tsp tartaric acid (sold as cream
    of tartar)
1 cup icing sugar
1 tsp baking soda
2 tbsp powdered fruit drink
    concentrate

Crush or grind citric and tartaric acids to a fine powder with a mortar and pestle or the back of a spoon.

Place all ingredients in a plastic bag and shake to combine. Store in an airtight container.

To make sherbet dabs, place sherbet into small paper lolly bags, add a stick candy or upside-down lollipop. Close the neck of the bag around the sweetie and seal with a sticker. The sherbet is then eaten by dipping the candy stick or lollipop into the sherbet then licking it off. These keep the kids busy and sticky through a movie or make a nice addition to party bags and family events.

Chocolate and nut Christmas trees

This edible Christmas centrepiece makes a great gift. To serve, place on a white platter surrounded by berries and let people snap pieces off at the end of the meal.

400 g dark chocolate
$^2/_3$ cup chopped dried apricots
$^2/_3$ cup sultanas
125 g slivered or
    chopped almonds
icing sugar, to dust
cellophane, to wrap

Prepare a pattern by drawing seven five-pointed stars inside circles on non-stick baking paper, starting at 16-cm diameter and reducing in size each time by 2 cm so you have the following size stars: 16 cm; 14 cm; 12 cm; 10 cm; 8 cm; 6 cm; and 4 cm. Outline the edges boldly. (These can be easily produced on a computer.)

Melt the chocolate gently in a large bowl. Add the fruit and nuts and mix well.

Cut out the stars and place on a baking sheet. Cover with baking paper – you should be able to see the outlines through the baking paper. Fill each star outline with chocolate mixture using a spoon and knife to mould the mixture into shape. Reserve enough of the mixture to stick the pieces together.

Put the stars in the fridge to firm up, then place a dab of the reserved mixture into the middle of the largest star. Stick the next largest on top, repeating the process using three of the stars, then refrigerate to harden before adding the remainder of the stars, in the same manner forming a tree. Refrigerate again, then dust lightly with icing sugar and wrap in cellophane.

Lollipops

Jewel-coloured star, heart and butterfly lollipops are impossible to resist.

1 cup sugar
¼ cup water
colouring and flavour
citric acid
ice-block sticks

In a medium saucepan, gently dissolve the sugar in the water. When dissolved, increase the heat until the mixture is boiling. Candy should boil evenly all over the surface — do not simmer. When mixture reaches soft-crack stage at aprroximately 140°C, add a couple of drops of colour and flavour. Continue boiling to hard-crack stage — 150°C on a candy thermometer. Remove from the heat and pour into a heatproof jug. Add a small pinch of citric acid then allow the bubbles to subside. Pour the candy into prepared moulds and allow to set. Store lollipops individually wrapped in cellophane in an airtight container.

Shaping and moulding hard candy

Lollipops can simply be dolloped onto a greased tray with an ice block stick pressed in as the candy sets. Plastic moulds can be used for individual sweeties; the plastic liners from the Christmas Advent calendars work well for sweeties or chocolate moulding (if using for chocolate moulding do not grease the moulds first, as greasing ruins the shine on the chocolate). Cookie cutters can also be wrapped in foil and greased to form a mould.

For fancy-shaped lollipops I have made moulds by rolling out play-dough or Plasticine and using cookie cutters to cut out shapes into which I pour the liquid candy to set.

Sometimes the candy can pick up a slight salty taste on the edges from the play-dough but this disappears after the first lick or can be avoided by dusting with caster sugar once the candy has set.

Hard candy is so
pretty and can
be coloured or
flavoured to suit
your taste . . .

THE BASICS

What everyone needs in their repertoire . . .

I'm not what you would call a 'morning person'. I can get up and get going when I have to. But, to be perfectly frank, I'd far rather spend 15 minutes extra in bed in the morning and then run around like I'm being chased by a swarm of bees, than get up earlier like a sane person.

So, when my kids hammer on the bedroom door at what feels like 4 am asking for a recipe because they want to make pancakes for breakfast for their friends who are at our house for a sleepover, I am less than amused. Even when I grunt at them to find the recipe themselves, they never take the hint.

I've noticed this about children, subtlety is lost on them. The fact that I have both eyes screwed tight shut and the duvet clamped around my neck has never worked as a deterrent. Rather, they leap onto the bed at most ungodly hours with their icy little feet and incessant chattering, and before long I've been sucked into their trap and I'm up making pancakes in my dressing gown with my morning hair scaring the daylights out of the visiting children — and my lovely warm bed grows cold.

I have often thought it would be good to gather together some of those basic recipes — the ones we carry in our heads or that are so frequently used or requested, that we don't really know where to find them anymore. For those mornings when the kids want to make pancakes or when my teenage nephews, who have over the years, airily declined all offers of culinary instruction, call me up in a panic on their rostered cooking night with a desperate, 'Aunt Soph, Aunt Soph, how do you make cheese sauce? And don't tell Mum I rang.'

The basics will vary somewhat from household to household but would probably include things that everyone needs in their repertoire: a good chocolate cake; an excellent cheese scone; and a selection of seasonings to add interest to a wide range of dishes.

Café pancakes

These pancakes are light and fluffy, and delicious with lashings of maple syrup. The recipe can be doubled or tripled depending on the number of people you are serving. The gluten-free version is just as light, fluffy and delicious as pancakes made with wheat flour.

Serves 4

1¼ cups plain flour
¼ cup sugar
2 tsp baking powder
pinch of salt
1 egg
¾ cup milk, soured with a squeeze
   of lemon juice
30 g butter, melted
extra butter or cooking spray,
   for cooking
maple syrup, to serve

Place the flour, sugar, baking powder and salt in a mixing bowl. Make a well in the centre and break in the egg. Add half the milk and use a whisk to mix, gradually incorporating the flour from around the sides of the bowl and adding the remainder of the milk a bit at a time to form a smooth batter. When all the flour has been incorporated, stir in the melted butter.

Heat two frying pans and melt a knob of butter in each or spray with cooking spray. Place generous spoonfuls of the mixture into the pans and cook gently until bubbles form over the surface of the pancakes. Turn and cook on the other side until springy and golden. Keep warm in the oven until all the mixture has been used. Serve warm with maple syrup.

Cook's tip
To make circular pancakes, pour the mixture off the end of the spoon rather than the side.

Gluten free
Use 1¼ cups gluten-free flour mix # 1, see page 12; 1 tsp guar gum.

Dairy free
Use approximately ¾ cup soy or rice milk soured with lemon juice. Use 1 tbsp non-dairy substitute instead of butter. Cook the pancakes in the same manner, but use a gentle heat to ensure they cook all the way through.

Really good cheese scones

A really good cheese scone is an excellent fast food. Make them up in bulk and freeze for lunch boxes, or bung a batch together to serve with soup or to toss into a picnic basket. Shaped into a round and scored into wedges, scone dough makes a good savoury bread, which is an excellent lunch with salad and maybe some cold meat or pickles.

FOR THE BASIC DOUGH
2 cups self-raising flour
2 cups grated cheese,
    extra for sprinkling
1¼ cups milk

Preheat the oven to 200°C.

Combine the flour, cheese and any other seasoning ingredients you fancy, see variations below, and mix well. Add the milk — the dough will be quite wet. Shape into small loaves or balls, sprinkle with extra cheese and bake for 10 minutes, until well risen and crusty. Serve warm or cold.

Variations
Add other flavours, such as cooked onion and bacon, chopped sun-dried tomatoes, chorizo, roasted capsicum, feta, and herbs. Try spreading some chutney or pesto over the top and adding a sprinkle of cheese before baking.

Cheese sauce

Pour this sauce over cooked vegetables, or a whole steamed cauliflower for cauliflower cheese, layer into a vegetable casserole or use to top a pasta bake.

3 tbsp butter
3 tbsp flour
400 ml milk
½ tsp salt
⅔ cup grated cheddar cheese

Melt the butter, and stir in the flour. While whisking continuously, add the milk a little at a time. Simmer gently, add the salt and cheese and stir until smooth.

Cook's tip
If you use trim milk don't let the sauce boil — it won't thicken properly. Using a whisk will ensure that you have a lump-free sauce.

Mac 'n' cheese

These days macaroni cheese is more likely to come from a packet or can than a hot pan but it's never been difficult to make. This is my version. You can omit the bacon or add fried onion. Some people like breadcrumbs or slices of tomato on the top — use this recipe as a base and create your own speciality.

Serves 4–6 as a light meal

400g dried macaroni elbows
   (or spirals or penne, if preferred)
75 g bacon, fat and rind removed,
   chopped in small pieces
1½ tbsp butter
1 tbsp oil
3 tbsp plain flour
700 ml reduced-fat milk
100 g grated cheese, plus a little
   extra for sprinkling
1 tbsp Parmesan cheese –
   it doesn't taste like it smells!
salt and pepper, to season

Preheat the oven to 190°C.

Bring 4 litres of water to the boil in a large saucepan, add a tsp of salt and boil the pasta for 10 minutes, according to manufacturer's instructions. While the pasta is cooking, prepare the sauce.

Cut the bacon into small pieces and cook it in a medium-sized saucepan. When the bacon is beginning to brown remove it from the pan and set it aside. Melt the butter and oil in the pan the bacon was cooked in, then use a whisk to mix the flour into the melted fats. Gradually whisk in the milk, adding it a little at a time, whisking well after each addition to ensure a lump-free sauce.

When all the milk has been added, return the bacon to the pan and using a wooden spoon stir the sauce over a gentle heat until it thickens. Don't let it boil and stir using circular and figure-of-eight motions so the sauce doesn't stick to the bottom of the pan. When it is thick enough to coat the back of the wooden spoon, stir in the grated cheese, Parmesan and salt and pepper. Taste to check the seasoning before stirring the cooked and drained pasta through the sauce. Tip the mixture into a heatproof dish, top with additional grated cheese and bake for 20 minutes, until golden on top.

DIY spice mixes

Make up these dried-spice mixes to use for seasoning marinades and meats, soups, sauces, spuds or anything else that needs a bit of zing. Mix well and store in airtight containers.

Cajun seasoning mix

This is excellent with grilled or barbecued meats, as a sprinkle on potato dishes or to season soups and stews.

1½ tbsp paprika
2 teaspoons salt
¼ tsp cayenne pepper
¼ tsp black pepper
1 tsp oregano
1 tsp thyme
1 tsp sugar

Tandoori mix

Combine with unsweetened natural yoghurt as a marinade for chicken, vegetable dishes with a mild curry flavour — or use as a dry spice-rub.

1 tbsp ground ginger
1 tbsp cumin
1 tbsp coriander
1 tbsp paprika
1 tbsp turmeric
1 tbsp salt
1 tbsp cayenne pepper
1 tbsp garam masala

Italian seasoning mix

Sprinkle over pizza bases, or use in sauces and pasta dishes.

3 tbsp dried oregano
2 tbsp dried thyme
2 tbsp dried marjoram
2 tbsp dried parsley
1 tsp black pepper

Mexican seasoning mix

This basic combination of flavours will add a Mexican zing to all sorts of dishes. Use as a sprinkle for spicy wedges, to season salsas, chilli and refried beans.

1 heaped tbsp ground cumin
2 tsp sugar
1 tsp salt
1 tsp oregano
1 tbsp chilli powder or flakes

Dana's chocolate cake

I believe this recipe is now one of the most frequently made recipes in the country. When people bring their cookbooks to dg cooking classes for me to sign, the page with Dana's chocolate cake is always the most splattered and tattered. I even had someone tell me she had made it for the Sultan of Brunei's household while doing a stint as their cook! The cake does rise high and sometimes cracks on top but always looks and tastes great. We also use it for shaped birthday cakes as it cuts neatly and freezes well, too.

FOR THE CAKE

1²/₃ cups flour

1½ cups sugar

²/₃ cup cocoa powder

1½ tsp baking soda

1 tsp salt

1½ cups of trim milk

100 g melted butter

2 eggs

1 tsp vanilla

FOR THE FROSTING

100 g butter

250 g icing sugar

1/₃ cup cocoa

milk to mix

1 tsp vanilla essence

Preheat oven to 180°C. Grease a 20-cm diameter cake tin and line the base with non-stick baking paper.

To make the cake, put all the ingredients into a processor and mix. Pour into the prepared tin and bake for at least 50 minutes, until the cake has risen, springs back when gently pressed, and a skewer poked into the centre of the cake comes out clean.

To make the frosting, place butter and dry ingredients in processor, pulse to combine, then add a dash of milk and pulse again. Continue until you achieve a soft spreadable icing, then add vanilla.

Slice the cake in half horizontally and spread some frosting on the bottom half. (You can also spread with jam or berry purée.) Replace the top half and cover the whole cake with frosting. Refrigerate to firm up the frosting.

Cook's tips

I get heaps of emails from people who believe I have mistakenly said baking soda when I mean baking powder. So why do we use baking soda not baking powder?

Both baking soda and baking powder are leavening agents added to baked goods before cooking to produce carbon dioxide and cause them to 'rise'. Baking powder contains baking soda, but the two substances are used under different conditions.

Baking soda is pure sodium bicarbonate. When it is combined with moisture and an acidic ingredient (e.g. yoghurt, chocolate, cocoa, buttermilk, honey), the resulting chemical reaction produces bubbles of carbon dioxide that expand under oven temperatures, causing baked goods to rise. The reaction begins immediately upon mixing the ingredients, so you need to bake the mixture promptly or it will fall flat.

Dana's gluten- and dairy-free chocolate cake

This recipe gets an A+ and reduced my daughter's coeliac and dairy-intolerant teacher to tears of delight when we made it for her. It makes a big, dark, chocolatey cake that slices well and doesn't seem to go instantly stale. It's a good kids' birthday cake or grown-ups' dessert cake.

FOR THE CAKE
2 cups gluten-free baking mix # 1
    (see page 12), extra if needed
2 tsp guar gum
1½ cups sugar
⅔ cup cocoa powder
1½ tsp baking soda
1 tsp salt
1 cup soy or rice milk or water
100 g non-dairy spread, melted
2 eggs
1 tsp vanilla essence

FOR THE FROSTING
250 g (about 1½ cups) gluten-free
    icing sugar (available from cake
    decorating suppliers)
100 g non-dairy spread, softened
⅓ cup cocoa
1 tsp vanilla essence
water to mix

Preheat oven to 180°C. Grease a 20-cm ring tin and line the base with non-stick baking paper.

Put all the ingredients for the cake into a processor and mix or combine in a bowl and beat until smooth — the batter should be thick but still able to be poured. Add more baking mix until the right texture is achieved. Pour into the prepared tin. Bake for at least 1 hour, until the cake has risen, springs back when gently pressed, and a skewer poked into the centre of the cake comes out clean.

To make the frosting, place icing sugar, non-dairy spread, cocoa and vanilla in a processor or bowl and combine. Add a dash of water and mix, continuing until you achieve a soft spreadable icing.

Slice the cake in half horizontally and spread some frosting on the bottom half. (You can also spread jam or berry purée.) Replace the top half and cover the whole cake with the frosting. Refrigerate to firm up the frosting.

Cook's tips
Use a ring tin when making gluten-free cakes as the mixture cannot stretch to support its own weight during rising.

Use high-quality baking cocoa with no starch or thickeners — I use Cadbury's Bourneville.

Egg allergy
I have successfully made this cake gluten and dairy free and, equally successfully, dairy and egg free, but when I tried to eliminate the gluten, dairy products and eggs it was nasty. You may have more success with a different flour blend — if so please let me know.

How to cook long-grain rice

Bring a large pot of water to the boil and add a good dash of iodised salt — salt adds flavour, buoyancy and iodine to the water. You need plenty of water as rice trebles in size as it cooks.

Stir in the rice, and cook in boiling water for 11 minutes. Drain the rice when cooked and rinse under hot water. Rinsing washes off the starch, most of which is released during cooking. The result is fluffy free-flowing rice. Place the drained rice on a platter in a warm oven for a few minutes before serving.

Cook's tip
In New Zealand, it is important to make sure you use iodised salt for cooking — iodine is an essential micronutrient not found in our food.

Roast potatoes

The best roast potatoes are crispy golden and sticky on the outside and fluffy inside. Drippings from a roast, chicken in particular, make the best and tastiest roast spuds. If I am not cooking a roast, I use a combination of olive oil and butter.

1 medium potato per person
   or more, if feeding teenagers
salt
1 slosh of oil
1 tbsp butter

Cook's tip
Choose a floury or all-purpose variety of potato for best results when roasting.

Preheat the oven to 200°C.

Peel the potatoes and cut into biggish, evenly sized pieces — too small and you will end up with all crispy crust and no fluffy spud.

Place the prepared potatoes in a large pot of cold water, add a pinch of salt and bring to the boil. Boil for 2–3 minutes then drain. Return the pot of potatoes to the heat to dry out, shaking the pot to turn the spuds and rough up the sides of the potatoes — scuffing them results in a crispier finish. Sprinkle lightly with salt.

If cooking a chicken or joint, pour off enough of the drippings to thinly coat the bottom of a shallow pan. If not roasting anything else then put the oil and butter into a large shallow roasting pan in the oven to heat, toss the potatoes into the hot pan and roll them around in the oil. Bake the spuds, turning occasionally, until crisp and golden.

Index

Credits

Thanks to the following stores for generously lending food photography props: Agnes Curran; Freedom Furniture, Wairau Park; Patty Baker and **Stevens** Newmarket; Providence; The Design Store; and Style Direct.

Page 106 — the Cayle Christmas cake's nutritional information was supplied by Diabetes Auckland, ph (09) 623 2508

Page 117 — The Alexander Turnbull Library holds a recorded typescript of Sarah Higgins's reminiscences. This extract was obtained from Sarah Ell's *Pioneer Women in New Zealand*, Auckland: Bush Press, 1992